TEXAS TEST PREP
Practice Test Book
STAAR Math
Grade 3

© 2014 by Test Master Press Texas

All rights reserved. No part of this book may be reproduced or transmitted in any form or by any means, electronic, mechanical, photocopying, recording, or otherwise without prior written permission.

ISBN 978-1502722157

CONTENTS

Introduction — 4

STAAR Mathematics: Practice Test 1 — 5
    Session 1 — 5
    Session 2 — 24

STAAR Mathematics: Practice Test 2 — 41
    Session 1 — 41
    Session 2 — 58

STAAR Mathematics: Practice Test 3 — 77
    Session 1 — 77
    Session 2 — 94

Answer Key — 112
    Practice Test 1: Session 1 — 113
    Practice Test 1: Session 2 — 116
    Practice Test 2: Session 1 — 119
    Practice Test 2: Session 2 — 122
    Practice Test 3: Session 1 — 125
    Practice Test 3: Session 2 — 128

Answer Sheets — 131
    Practice Test 1 — 131
    Practice Test 2 — 132
    Practice Test 3 — 133

STAAR Grade 3 Mathematics Reference Sheet — 134

INTRODUCTION
For Parents, Teachers, and Tutors

About the STAAR Assessments and the Revised TEKS Skills

Students in Texas will be assessed each year by taking a set of tests known as the State of Texas Assessments of Academic Readiness, or STAAR. Beginning with the 2014-2015 school year, the assessments will cover the skills listed in the revised TEKS for mathematics. The questions in this book cover all the skills in the revised TEKS and will prepare students for the 2014-2015 STAAR assessments.

About the Practice Tests

This practice test book contains three complete STAAR Mathematics tests. Each test contains 60 questions. This is slightly more than the actual tests that contain 46 questions. The extra questions will ensure that students have practice with all the skills assessed on the actual state test.

Types of Questions

The majority of the test is made up of multiple-choice questions. Students can answer the questions by filling in the circle of their answer choice in the test book. Students can also answer the questions by filling in the circles on the answer sheet in the back of the book. The test also contains several gridded-response questions where students write their answers in a grid.

Timing the Test

Students are given 4 hours to complete the actual STAAR mathematics test. This can be divided into two or more sessions, but all sessions are always completed on the same day. The practice tests in this book have been divided into two sessions. To account for the extra questions, students should be able to complete each session in 2.5 hours. You can use this time limit, or you can choose not to time the test.

Calculators and Tools

Students should be provided with a ruler to use on both sessions of the test. Students are not allowed to use a calculator on any session of the STAAR tests, and so should complete all the practice tests without the use of a calculator.

STAAR Mathematics

Grade 3

Practice Test 1

Session 1

Directions

Read each question carefully. For a multiple-choice question, determine the best answer to the question from the four answer choices provided.

For a griddable question, determine the best answer. Write your answer at the top of the grid. Then shade the grid to show your answer.

You may use a ruler to help you answer questions. You may also use the information on the Reference Sheet at the back of this book. You may not use a calculator on this test.

1   There are 1,920 students at Jenna's school. Which of these is another way to write 1,920?

   Ⓐ   1,000 + 900 + 20

   Ⓑ   1,000 + 900 + 2

   Ⓒ   1,000 + 90 + 20

   Ⓓ   1,000 + 90 + 2

2   The graph shows the number of points six players scored in a basketball game.

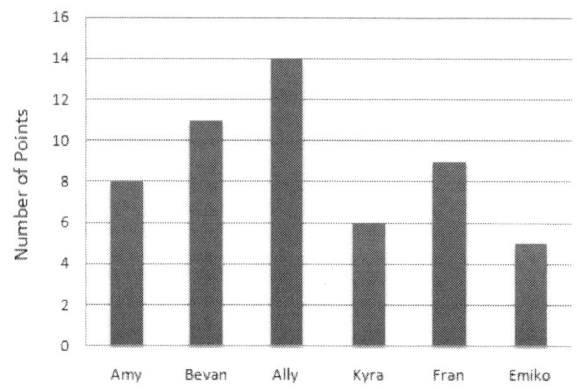

How many points did Kyra and Fran score together?

   Ⓐ   6

   Ⓑ   9

   Ⓒ   15

   Ⓓ   16

3 What do the shaded models below show?

Ⓐ $\frac{5}{8} > \frac{1}{2}$

Ⓑ $\frac{5}{8} = \frac{1}{2}$

Ⓒ $\frac{5}{8} < \frac{4}{8}$

Ⓓ $\frac{5}{8} > \frac{1}{5}$

4 Bianca's father sold 182 pretzels on Saturday. Then he sold 218 pretzels on Sunday. Each pretzel sold for $2. Which expression could be used to find how much money Bianca's father made in all?

Ⓐ   182 + 218 × $2

Ⓑ   182 × 218 × $2

Ⓒ   182 + (218 × $2)

Ⓓ   (182 + 218) × $2

5   Michael drove 1,285 miles during a vacation. Which digit is in the tens place in the number 1,285?

    Ⓐ   1
    Ⓑ   2
    Ⓒ   8
    Ⓓ   5

6   Donna has 18 roses. She wants to put the roses into vases so that each vase has the same number of roses, with no roses left over.

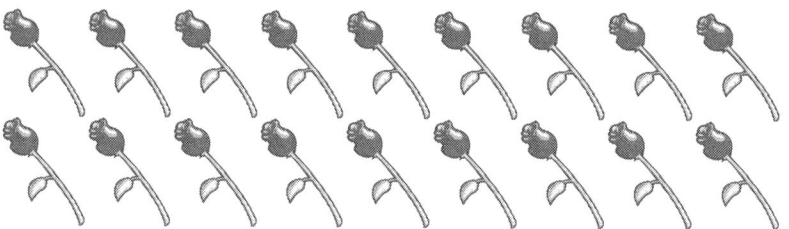

    How many roses could Donna put in each vase?

    Ⓐ   4
    Ⓑ   5
    Ⓒ   6
    Ⓓ   8

7 Which group shows that $\frac{1}{4}$ of the stars are shaded?

Ⓐ

Ⓑ

Ⓒ

Ⓓ

8   Patrick bought 2 packets of pencils for $4 per packet. He also bought 3 packets of crayons for $3 per packet. How much did Patrick spend in all, in dollars? Record your answer and fill in the bubbles on the grid. Be sure to use the correct place value.

9 Each square on the grid below is 1 cm wide and 1 cm high.

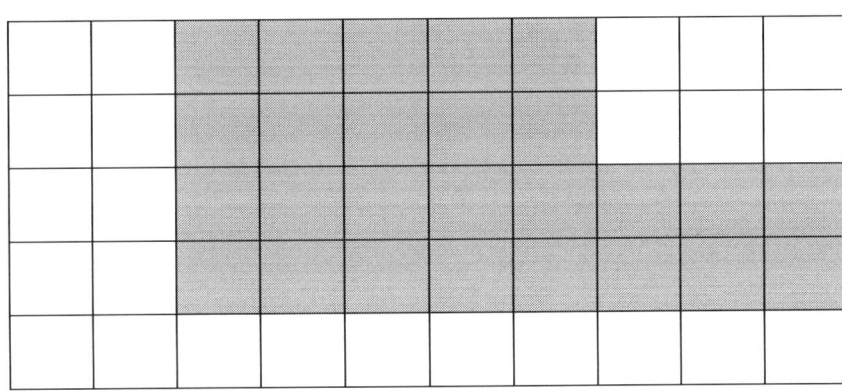

Which expression could be used to find the area of the shaded figure?

Ⓐ (5 x 4) + (3 x 2)

Ⓑ (10 x 5) – (5 x 6)

Ⓒ (8 x 2) + (5 x 4)

Ⓓ (8 x 4) – 3

10 Billy collects pennies and nickels. Billy has 142 pennies and 56 nickels in his coin collection. Which is the best estimate of the total number of coins in Billy's collection?

Ⓐ 150

Ⓑ 180

Ⓒ 200

Ⓓ 250

11 Squares and rectangles are quadrilaterals. Which of the shapes below is also a quadrilateral?

Ⓐ

Ⓑ

Ⓒ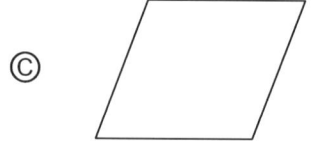

Ⓓ

12 Ribbon costs $4 per yard. Allie buys 16 yards of ribbon. Which number sentence could be used to find the total cost of the ribbon, *c*, in dollars?

Ⓐ 16 + 4 = c

Ⓑ 16 − 4 = c

Ⓒ 16 × 4 = c

Ⓓ 16 ÷ 4 = c

13 What value for *x* makes the equation below true?

$$54 \div x = 9$$

Record your answer and fill in the bubbles on the grid. Be sure to use the correct place value.

14 Margaret folded the net shown below to make a shape.

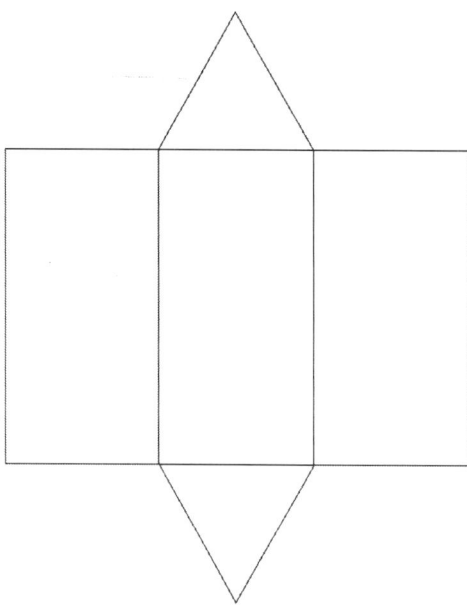

What shape did Margaret make?

- Ⓐ Triangular prism
- Ⓑ Triangular pyramid
- Ⓒ Rectangular prism
- Ⓓ Rectangular pyramid

15 Leonard finds the capacity of the pool. What does the capacity of the pool tell Leonard?

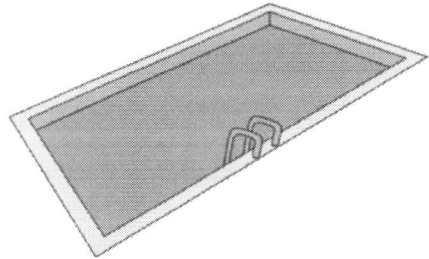

- Ⓐ How deep the pool is
- Ⓑ How far he would swim with each lap
- Ⓒ The distance around the edge of the pool
- Ⓓ The amount of water it takes to fill the pool

16 Kira was asked to make a number using only the digits 1, 5, 8, and 9. She could only use each digit once. What is the largest number Kira could make?

- Ⓐ 1,589
- Ⓑ 9,581
- Ⓒ 9,851
- Ⓓ 9,815

17 The table shows how many people saw a play each night.

Day	Number of People
Friday	225
Saturday	342
Sunday	290

Which number sentence shows the best estimate of the total number of people who saw the play?

Ⓐ   200 + 300 + 200 = 700

Ⓑ   200 + 300 + 300 = 800

Ⓒ   200 + 400 + 300 = 900

Ⓓ   300 + 400 + 300 = 1,000

18 What fraction of the coins shown below are quarters?

Ⓐ $\frac{1}{2}$

Ⓑ $\frac{1}{3}$

Ⓒ $\frac{2}{3}$

Ⓓ $\frac{3}{5}$

19 Which number sentence represents the array shown below?

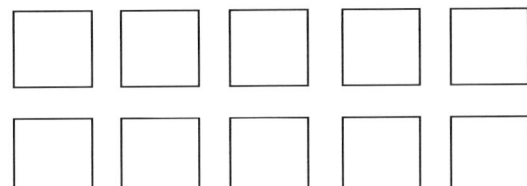

- Ⓐ 5 + 2 = 7
- Ⓑ 5 × 5 = 25
- Ⓒ 5 × 2 = 10
- Ⓓ 5 − 2 = 3

20 Which point on the number line represents $1\frac{3}{4}$?

- Ⓐ Point F
- Ⓑ Point G
- Ⓒ Point H
- Ⓓ Point J

21   David filled the bucket below with water.

About how much water would it take to fill the bucket?
- Ⓐ   5 milliliters
- Ⓑ   5 pints
- Ⓒ   5 liters
- Ⓓ   5 quarts

22   Leah has 3 pies. She cut each pie into 8 pieces.

How many pieces of pie does Leah have?
- Ⓐ   24
- Ⓑ   16
- Ⓒ   18
- Ⓓ   32

23 Which shape has more sides than a pentagon?

Ⓐ Triangle

Ⓑ Square

Ⓒ Hexagon

Ⓓ Rectangle

24 A dollar bill has a length of 156 mm and a height of 66 mm.

Which is the best estimate of the perimeter of a dollar bill?

Ⓐ 230 mm

Ⓑ 300 mm

Ⓒ 460 mm

Ⓓ 600 mm

25 What is the area of the square below?

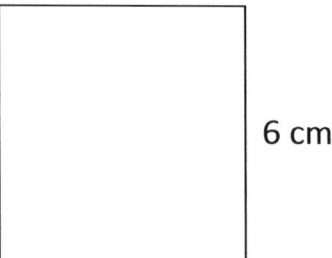

6 cm

- Ⓐ 12 cm²
- Ⓑ 24 cm²
- Ⓒ 30 cm²
- Ⓓ 36 cm²

26 Look at the numbers below.

21 17 15 9

Which of these describes all the numbers?

- Ⓐ They can all be divided evenly by 3.
- Ⓑ They are all odd numbers.
- Ⓒ They are all 2-digit numbers.
- Ⓓ They are all less than 20.

27 Andrew is selling muffins at a bake sale. The table shows the profit he makes by selling 5, 10, 15, and 20 muffins.

Muffins Sold	Profit Made
5	$15
10	$30
15	$45
20	$60

Based on the table above, how much profit does Andrew make for selling 1 muffin?

Ⓐ $15

Ⓑ $5

Ⓒ $3

Ⓓ $2

28 Kai found the coins shown below in the sofa. What is the value of the coins that Kai found?

Ⓐ $1.26

Ⓑ $1.36

Ⓒ $1.45

Ⓓ $2.36

29 Mario buys screws in packets of 6.

If Mario counts the screws in groups of 6, which number could he **NOT** count?

Ⓐ 30

Ⓑ 16

Ⓒ 24

Ⓓ 18

30 Mrs. Bowen cooked dinner for 24 guests. She cooked 3 courses for each guest. Which equation shows how many courses Mrs. Bowen cooked?

Ⓐ 24 × 3 = 72

Ⓑ 24 + 3 = 27

Ⓒ 24 − 3 = 21

Ⓓ 24 ÷ 3 = 8

END OF SESSION 1

STAAR Mathematics

Grade 3

Practice Test 1

Session 2

Directions

Read each question carefully. For a multiple-choice question, determine the best answer to the question from the four answer choices provided.

For a griddable question, determine the best answer. Write your answer at the top of the grid. Then shade the grid to show your answer.

You may use a ruler to help you answer questions. You may also use the information on the Reference Sheet at the back of this book. You may not use a calculator on this test.

31 In which number sentence does the number 8 make the equation true?

Ⓐ   48 ÷ ☐ = 6

Ⓑ   ☐ ÷ 6 = 48

Ⓒ   48 × 6 = ☐

Ⓓ   ☐ × 48 = 6

32 The graph below shows the high temperature for five days.

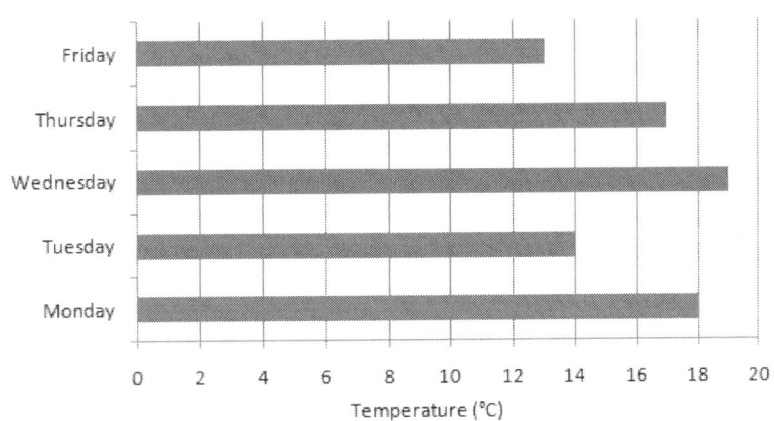

On which day was the high temperature 17°C?

Ⓐ   Tuesday

Ⓑ   Wednesday

Ⓒ   Thursday

Ⓓ   Friday

33 Which model is shaded to show a fraction equivalent to $\frac{6}{8}$?

Ⓐ
Ⓑ
Ⓒ
Ⓓ

34 Beads are sold in packets of 6 or packets of 8. Liz needs to buy exactly 30 beads. Which set of packets could Liz buy?

Ⓐ 1 packet of 8 beads and 2 packets of 6 beads

Ⓑ 2 packets of 8 beads and 2 packets of 6 beads

Ⓒ 1 packet of 8 beads and 3 packets of 6 beads

Ⓓ 3 packets of 8 beads and 1 packet of 6 beads

35 Joy had $18. She bought a pair of shorts for $11. Then she bought a scarf for $3. Which expression shows one way to find how much money Joy had left?

Ⓐ 18 + 11 + 3

Ⓑ 18 + 11 − 3

Ⓒ 18 − 11 + 3

Ⓓ 18 − 11 − 3

36 Which point on the number line represents 80?

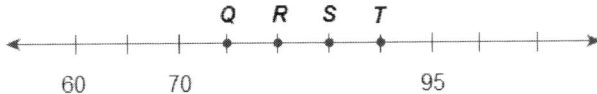

- Ⓐ Point Q
- Ⓑ Point R
- Ⓒ Point S
- Ⓓ Point T

37 The graph below shows how long Jody studied each week day.

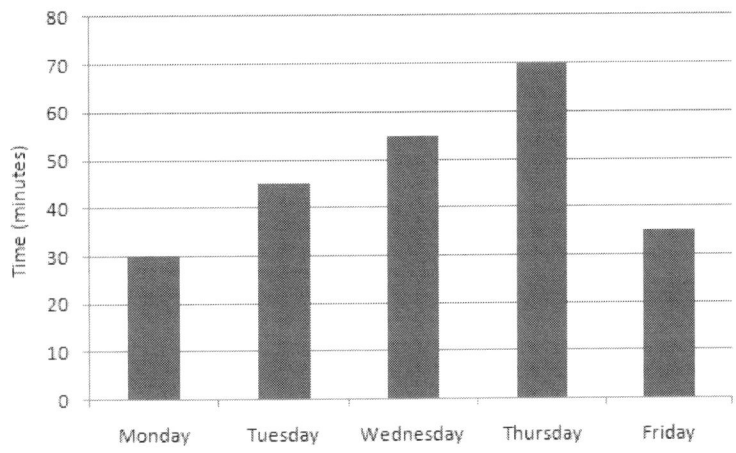

On which day did Jody study for between 40 and 50 minutes?

- Ⓐ Tuesday
- Ⓑ Wednesday
- Ⓒ Thursday
- Ⓓ Friday

Practice Test Book, STAAR Math, Grade 3

38 Reggie arrived at the train station at the time shown below.

Reggie's train left 30 minutes after that time. What time did Reggie's train leave?

Ⓐ 1:15

Ⓑ 1:45

Ⓒ 3:15

Ⓓ 3:45

39 Davis made a pictograph to show how many letters three students wrote in a month. Bobby wrote 8 letters. How many letter symbols should Davis use to show 8 letters?

Davis	✉✉✉
Bobby	
Inga	✉✉

Each ✉ means 2 letters.

Ⓐ 8

Ⓑ 4

Ⓒ 2

Ⓓ 16

28

40 Bindu is slicing apples into 8 slices. Which table shows how many apple slices Bindu will have if she uses 2, 4, and 5 apples?

Ⓐ
Number of Apples	Number of Slices
2	16
4	32
5	40

Ⓑ
Number of Apples	Number of Slices
2	8
4	32
5	40

Ⓒ
Number of Apples	Number of Slices
2	8
4	32
5	20

Ⓓ
Number of Apples	Number of Slices
2	10
4	20
5	25

41 The graph below shows how long Jason studied for one week.

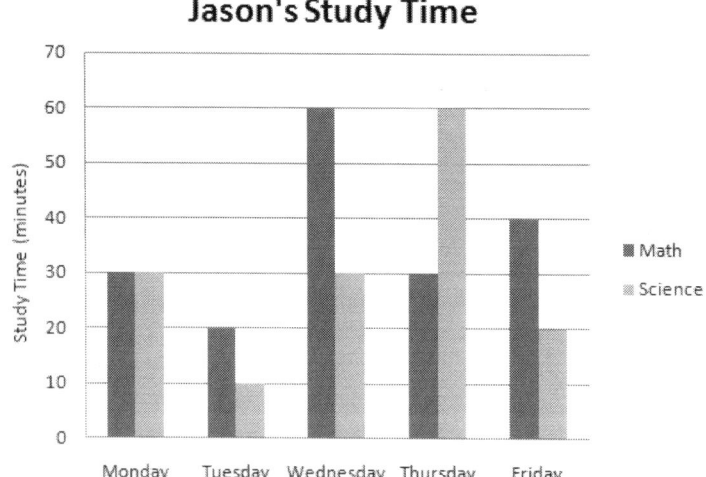

How long did Jason study science for on Thursday?

Ⓐ   30 minutes

Ⓑ   60 minutes

Ⓒ   90 minutes

Ⓓ   20 minutes

42 What is the product of 8 and 9? Record your answer and fill in the bubbles on the grid. Be sure to use the correct place value.

43 Andy was buying a used car. He had four cars to choose from. The four cars had the odometer readings below.

Car	Chrysler	Ford	Honda	Saturn
Reading (miles)	22,482	21,987	23,689	22,501

If Andy decided to buy the car with the second highest odometer reading, which car would be buy?

Ⓐ   Chrysler

Ⓑ   Ford

Ⓒ   Honda

Ⓓ   Saturn

44 The table below shows the entry cost for a museum.

Adult	$10 per person
Child	$8 per person
Family (2 adults and 2 children)	$30 per family

How much would a family of 2 adults and 2 children save by buying a family ticket instead of individual tickets?

Ⓐ $2
Ⓑ $6
Ⓒ $8
Ⓓ $10

45 Josephine boarded a train at 10:40 a.m. She got off the train at 11:35 a.m. How long was she on the train for?

Ⓐ   45 minutes
Ⓑ   55 minutes
Ⓒ   65 minutes
Ⓓ   95 minutes

46 What is the area of the shaded figure on the grid below?

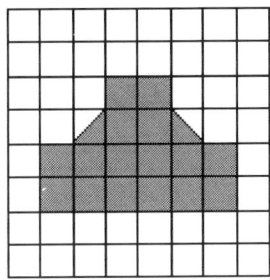

Ⓐ 17 square units

Ⓑ 16 square units

Ⓒ 18 square units

Ⓓ 24 square units

47 Which fraction model is equivalent to $\frac{1}{2}$?

Ⓐ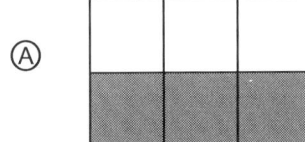

Ⓑ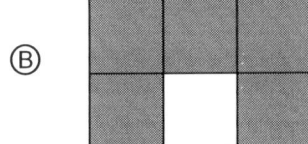

Ⓒ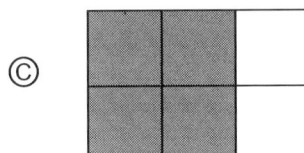

Ⓓ

48 Sally is making a pictograph to show how many students are in grade 3, grade 4, and grade 5.

Grade 3	☺☺☺☺☺☺☺☺☺☺☺
Grade 4	☺☺☺☺☺☺☺☺☺☺☺☺
Grade 5	

☺ = 5 students

There are 65 students in grade 5. How many ☺ symbols should Sally use to represent the students in grade 5? Record your answer and fill in the bubbles on the grid. Be sure to use the correct place value.

49 Which of the following describes a rectangle?

- Ⓐ 3 pairs of parallel faces
- Ⓑ 6 vertices
- Ⓒ 4 acute angles
- Ⓓ 2 pairs of congruent sides

50 What fraction of the model is shaded?

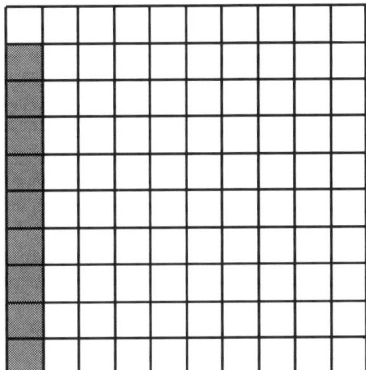

- Ⓐ $\frac{1}{9}$
- Ⓑ $\frac{9}{10}$
- Ⓒ $\frac{9}{91}$
- Ⓓ $\frac{9}{100}$

51 Which of these is equal to $\frac{1}{5} + \frac{1}{5} + \frac{1}{5}$?

Ⓐ $\frac{3}{5}$

Ⓑ $\frac{3}{15}$

Ⓒ $\frac{1}{15}$

Ⓓ $\frac{1}{125}$

52 Which number makes the number sentence below true?

$$18 \times \boxed{} = 18$$

Ⓐ 0

Ⓑ 1

Ⓒ 10

Ⓓ 18

53 Which fraction is represented by point *Y*?

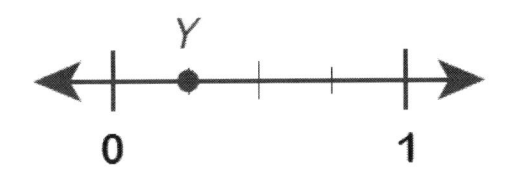

- Ⓐ $\dfrac{1}{3}$
- Ⓑ $\dfrac{1}{4}$
- Ⓒ $\dfrac{1}{5}$
- Ⓓ $\dfrac{1}{8}$

54 Which of these is another way of expressing 6 × 14?
- Ⓐ (6 × 10) + (6 × 4)
- Ⓑ (6 × 1) + (6 × 4)
- Ⓒ (6 × 10) + 4
- Ⓓ (6 × 4) + 10

55 Oliver earns $12 per hour. How many hours will Oliver have to work to earn $600 per week?
- Ⓐ 40 hours
- Ⓑ 45 hours
- Ⓒ 50 hours
- Ⓓ 55 hours

56 Which statement is true of all even numbers?

    Ⓐ   They can be divided evenly by 2.

    Ⓑ   They can be divided evenly by 4.

    Ⓒ   They can be divided evenly by 5.

    Ⓓ   They can be divided evenly by 10.

57 What is the shape of the can shown below?

    Ⓐ   Cone

    Ⓑ   Cylinder

    Ⓒ   Sphere

    Ⓓ   Pyramid

58 Which measurement best tells the amount of liquid the water bowl below holds?

- Ⓐ Capacity
- Ⓑ Weight
- Ⓒ Height
- Ⓓ Length

59 Troy swapped 2 quarters for coins with the same value. Which of these could Troy have swapped his 2 quarters for?

- Ⓐ 25 pennies
- Ⓑ 20 nickels
- Ⓒ 10 nickels
- Ⓓ 10 dimes

60 Hannah collects data on education level and annual salary. Hannah uses the data to make a line graph. What trend would most likely be seen?

Ⓐ Annual salary would decrease as education level increases.

Ⓑ Annual salary would increase as education level increases.

Ⓒ Annual salary would remain the same even as education level increases.

Ⓓ There would be no relationship between education level and annual salary.

END OF TEST

STAAR Mathematics

Grade 3

Practice Test 2

Session 1

Directions

Read each question carefully. For a multiple-choice question, determine the best answer to the question from the four answer choices provided.

For a griddable question, determine the best answer. Write your answer at the top of the grid. Then shade the grid to show your answer.

You may use a ruler to help you answer questions. You may also use the information on the Reference Sheet at the back of this book. You may not use a calculator on this test.

1. There are 30,804 people living in Montville. Which of these is another way to write 30,804?

   Ⓐ   30,000 + 800 + 4

   Ⓑ   30 + 80 + 4

   Ⓒ   3,000 + 800 + 40

   Ⓓ   300 + 80 + 4

2. The graph below shows the number of pets four girls have.

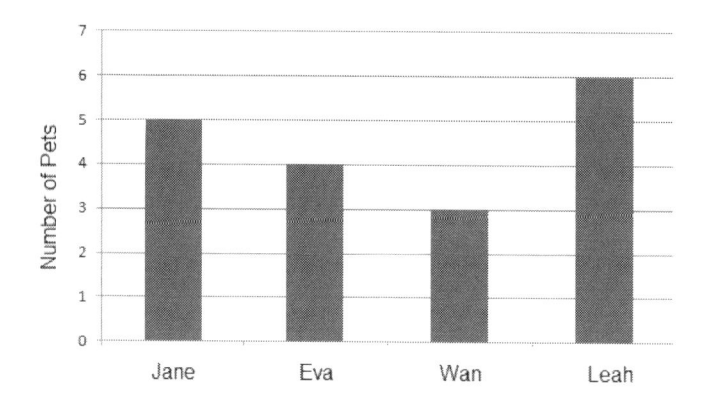

   Which two girls have 10 pets in total?

   Ⓐ   Jane and Eva

   Ⓑ   Wan and Leah

   Ⓒ   Eva and Leah

   Ⓓ   Leah and Jane

3 Which point on the number line represents 48?

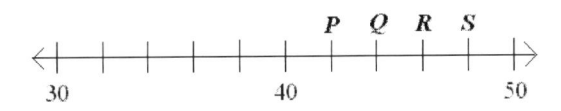

```
              P  Q  R  S
  ←+--+--+--+--+--+--+--+--+→
   30          40          50
```

Ⓐ   Point *P*

Ⓑ   Point *Q*

Ⓒ   Point *R*

Ⓓ   Point *S*

4 Rory scored 28 points in a basketball game. Adam scored 4 points less than Rory. Danny scored 6 points more than Adam. How many points did Danny score?

Ⓐ   18

Ⓑ   30

Ⓒ   26

Ⓓ   38

5   There were 17,856 people living in Eastwood in 2009. What is the value of the digit 8 in 17,856?

   Ⓐ   Eight hundred

   Ⓑ   Eight thousand

   Ⓒ   Eighty thousand

   Ⓓ   Eighty

6   Chan had a bag of 28 lollipops. He divided the lollipops evenly between several children.

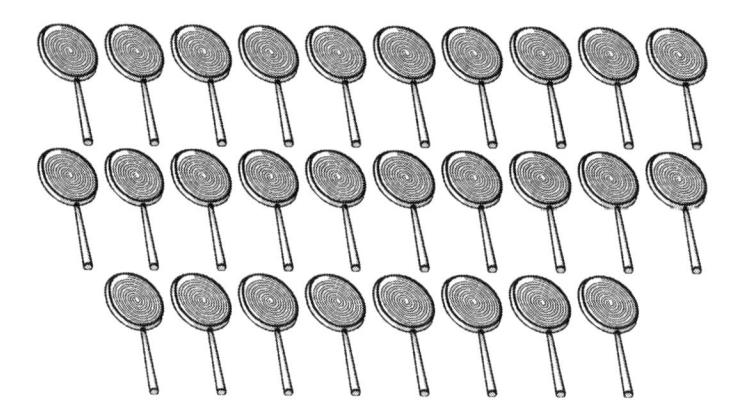

   If there were no lollipops left over, how many lollipops could each child have received?

   Ⓐ   6

   Ⓑ   7

   Ⓒ   8

   Ⓓ   9

7 Rory began studying one evening at the time shown on the clock below.

He studied for 1 hour and 20 minutes. What time did he finish studying?

Ⓐ   7:15 p.m.

Ⓑ   7:55 p.m.

Ⓒ   8:05 p.m.

Ⓓ   8:15 p.m.

8 Ally bought 3 packets of pencils and 2 packets of pens. There were 8 pencils in each packet, and 6 pens in each packet. Which expression could be used to find how many more pencils she bought than pens?

Ⓐ   (8 × 6) − (3 × 2)

Ⓑ   (8 − 3) × (6 − 2)

Ⓒ   (3 × 8) − (2 × 6)

Ⓓ   (3 + 8) − (2 + 6)

9 Georgia made the design below.

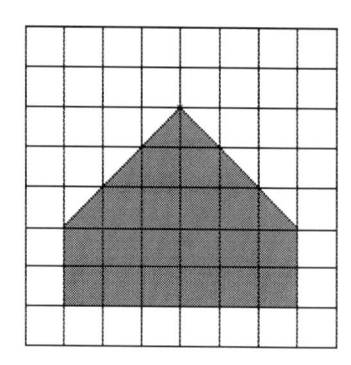

Each square on the grid measures 1 square centimeter. What is the area of the shaded part of the design?

Ⓐ   21 square centimeters

Ⓑ   24 square centimeters

Ⓒ   18 square centimeters

Ⓓ   20 square centimeters

10 Ling scored 82 on a reading test. Mickey scored 63 on the reading test. Which is the best estimate of how many more points Ling scored than Mickey?

Ⓐ   10

Ⓑ   15

Ⓒ   20

Ⓓ   25

11. Sushi sells for $3 for each small roll and $5 for each large roll. Derrick bought 4 small rolls and 7 large rolls. How much did Derrick spend in all, in dollars? Record your answer and fill in the bubbles on the grid. Be sure to use the correct place value.

12 A diner has 18 tables. Each table can seat 4 people. The diner also has 8 benches that can each seat 6 people. How many people can the diner seat in all?

- Ⓐ 36
- Ⓑ 120
- Ⓒ 260
- Ⓓ 308

13 Which shape has fewer sides than a pentagon?

- Ⓐ Heptagon
- Ⓑ Square
- Ⓒ Hexagon
- Ⓓ Octagon

14 What is the product of 8 and 7?

- Ⓐ 49
- Ⓑ 52
- Ⓒ 56
- Ⓓ 64

15 Which number goes in the box to make the equation below true?

$$54 \div \boxed{} = 9$$

Ⓐ 6
Ⓑ 7
Ⓒ 8
Ⓓ 9

16 The grade 3 students at Sam's school are collecting cans for a food drive. The table below shows how many cans each class collected.

Class	Number of Cans
Miss Powell	39
Mr. Sato	42
Mrs. Joshi	26
Mr. Perez	37

Which number sentence shows the best estimate of the total number of cans collected?

Ⓐ 40 + 40 + 30 + 40 = 150
Ⓑ 40 + 40 + 20 + 40 = 140
Ⓒ 40 + 40 + 20 + 30 = 130
Ⓓ 30 + 40 + 20 + 30 = 120

17 On Monday, there were 21 students in a dance class. There were 4 students missing from the class. How many students are usually in the dance class?

- Ⓐ 17
- Ⓑ 19
- Ⓒ 21
- Ⓓ 25

18 Janine bought a packet of muffins. The packet contained 4 chocolate muffins and 2 vanilla muffins.

What fraction of the muffins were vanilla?

- Ⓐ $\frac{1}{2}$
- Ⓑ $\frac{1}{3}$
- Ⓒ $\frac{2}{3}$
- Ⓓ $\frac{3}{5}$

19 During a season with little rainfall, the amount of pumpkins grown is much less than usual. What would this most likely lead to?

Ⓐ Lower prices for pumpkins

Ⓑ Higher prices for pumpkins

Ⓒ More people wanting to buy pumpkins

Ⓓ More pumpkins being wasted

20 Look at the number line below.

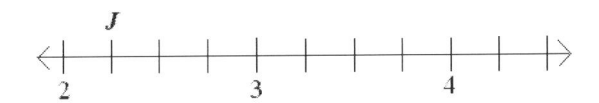

What fraction does point *J* represent?

Ⓐ $2\frac{1}{4}$

Ⓑ $2\frac{1}{3}$

Ⓒ $2\frac{1}{5}$

Ⓓ $2\frac{1}{2}$

21 How many vertices does the square pyramid shown below have?

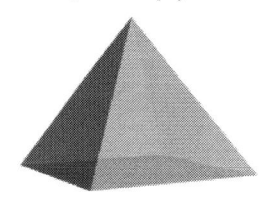

Ⓐ 4
Ⓑ 5
Ⓒ 6
Ⓓ 8

22 A pizza has 8 slices.

Eriko wants to order enough pizza to have at least 62 slices. What is the least number of pizzas Eriko could order?

Ⓐ 7
Ⓑ 8
Ⓒ 9
Ⓓ 10

23 Which figure below is a trapezoid?

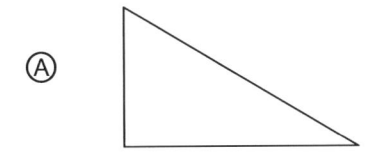

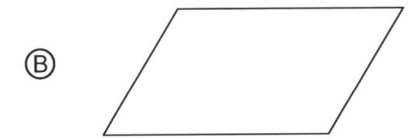

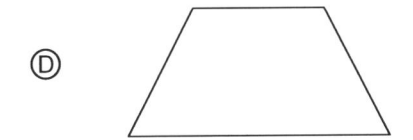

Ⓐ

Ⓑ

Ⓒ

Ⓓ

24 The population of Greenville is 609,023. What does the 9 in this number represent?

Ⓐ Nine thousand

Ⓑ Ninety thousand

Ⓒ Nine hundred thousand

Ⓓ Ninety

25 Habib measured the length of each wall of his room. A diagram of Habib's room is shown below.

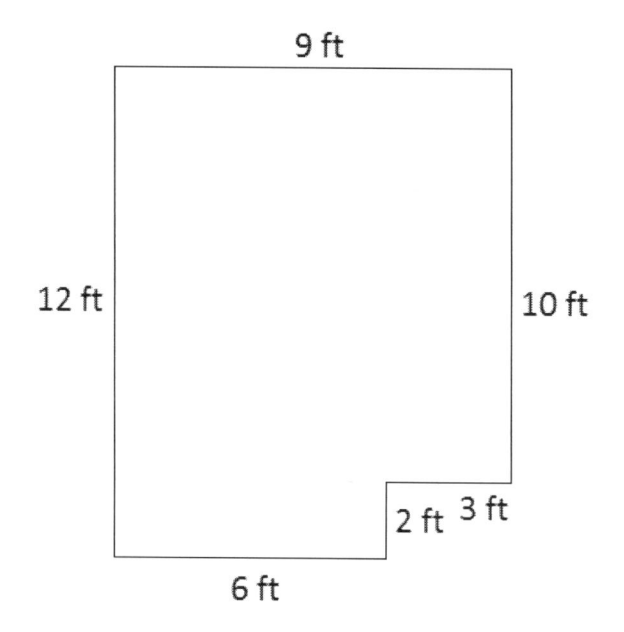

```
           9 ft
      ┌──────────┐
      │          │
      │          │
12 ft │          │ 10 ft
      │          │
      │       ┌──┘
      │       │ 2 ft  3 ft
      └───────┘
         6 ft
```

What is the perimeter of Habib's room?

Ⓐ 37 ft

Ⓑ 40 ft

Ⓒ 39 ft

Ⓓ 42 ft

26   Which point on the number line represents 44?

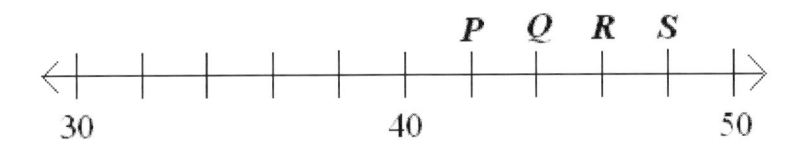

         P   Q   R   S
    ←|—|—|—|—|—|—|—|—|—|→
     30   40   50

   Ⓐ   Point P
   Ⓑ   Point Q
   Ⓒ   Point R
   Ⓓ   Point S

27   Apples are sold in bags. There are the same number of apples in each bag. The table below shows the number of apples in 2, 3, and 4 bags.

Number of Bags	Number of Apples
2	12
3	18
4	24
6	

Based on the table above, how many apples are in 6 bags?

   Ⓐ   30
   Ⓑ   28
   Ⓒ   36
   Ⓓ   42

28 Mia bought a milkshake. She was given the change shown below. How much change was Mia given?

Ⓐ $0.76

Ⓑ $0.71

Ⓒ $0.51

Ⓓ $0.66

29 Toni has tokens for arcade games.

If Toni counts her tokens in groups of 6, which list shows only numbers she would count?

- Ⓐ 6, 8, 10, 12
- Ⓑ 6, 10, 16, 20
- Ⓒ 12, 18, 24, 30
- Ⓓ 12, 16, 20, 24

30 Damon is 51 inches tall. Alka is 57 inches tall. Gemma is 49 inches tall. Which of the following compares the heights correctly?

- Ⓐ 49 < 51 < 57
- Ⓑ 57 < 51 < 49
- Ⓒ 49 < 57 < 51
- Ⓓ 57 > 51 < 49

END OF SESSION 1

STAAR Mathematics

Grade 3

Practice Test 2

Session 2

Directions

Read each question carefully. For a multiple-choice question, determine the best answer to the question from the four answer choices provided.

For a griddable question, determine the best answer. Write your answer at the top of the grid. Then shade the grid to show your answer.

You may use a ruler to help you answer questions. You may also use the information on the Reference Sheet at the back of this book. You may not use a calculator on this test.

31 Which number is greater than 5,167?

    Ⓐ   5,096

    Ⓑ   5,203

    Ⓒ   5,159

    Ⓓ   5,164

32 Emma grouped a set of numbers into two groups. The groups are shown below.

Group 1	Group 2
14	21
86	79
922	325
388	683

Which number belongs in Group 2?

    Ⓐ   18

    Ⓑ   630

    Ⓒ   864

    Ⓓ   247

33 Look at the group of numbers below.

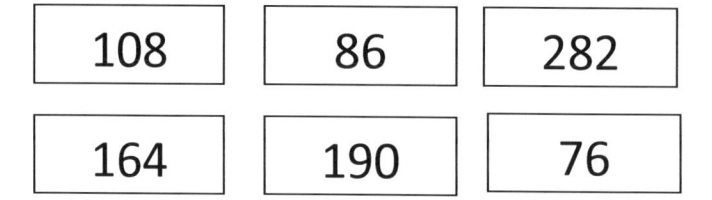

108	86	282
164	190	76

What do these numbers have in common?

Ⓐ They are all even numbers.

Ⓑ They are all odd numbers.

Ⓒ They are all greater than 100.

Ⓓ They are all less than 200.

34 There are 30 students in a class. The teacher needs to divide the students in the class into teams. Each team must have the same number of students in it. There cannot be any students left over. Which of the following could describe the teams?

Ⓐ 7 teams of 4 students

Ⓑ 8 teams of 4 students

Ⓒ 6 teams of 5 students

Ⓓ 10 teams of 2 students

35 When Travis got on a bus, there were 16 people on the bus. After the first stop, there were 4 times as many people on the bus. Which expression can be used to find the number of people on the bus after the first stop?

- Ⓐ 16 × 4
- Ⓑ 16 ÷ 4
- Ⓒ 16 − 4
- Ⓓ 16 + 4

36 The table below shows the cost of hiring CDs, DVDs, and video games from a hire store.

Item	Cost per Week
CD	$2
DVD	$3
Video game	$4

Zola hired 5 items for 1 week. The total cost was exactly $16. Which items could Zola have hired?

- Ⓐ 1 CD, 2 DVDs, 2 video games
- Ⓑ 1 CD, 3 DVDs, 1 video game
- Ⓒ 2 CDs, 1 DVD, 2 video games
- Ⓓ 2 CDs, 2 DVDs, 1 video game

37 The pictograph shows how many emails Sammy received each week day.

Monday	✉✉✉
Tuesday	✉✉
Wednesday	✉✉✉✉
Thursday	✉✉✉
Friday	✉✉✉✉✉✉

Each ✉ means 2 emails.

How many emails did Sammy receive on Wednesday?

Ⓐ 8

Ⓑ 6

Ⓒ 4

Ⓓ 3

38 Which number sentence represents the array shown below?

Ⓐ 5 + 4 = 9

Ⓑ 5 × 5 = 25

Ⓒ 5 × 4 = 20

Ⓓ 5 − 4 = 1

39 Naomi is making a pictograph to show how many fruit trees there are in her yard. The pictograph she has made so far is shown below.

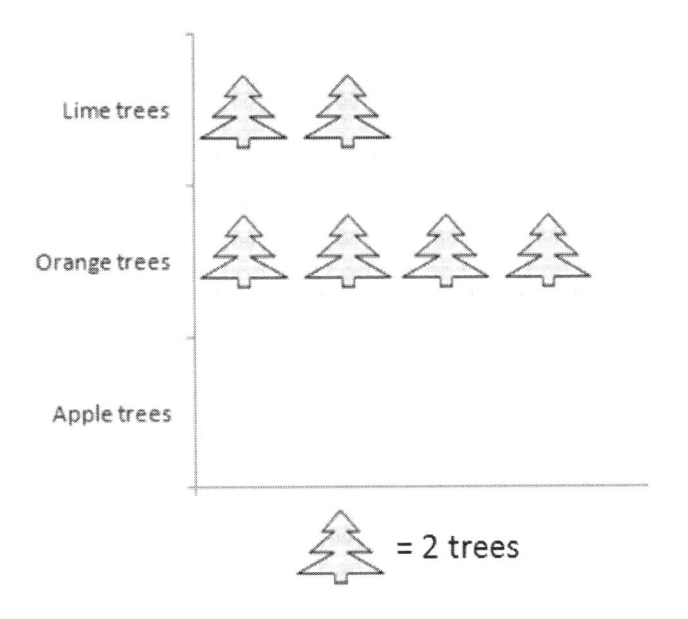

Lime trees: 🌲 🌲
Orange trees: 🌲 🌲 🌲 🌲
Apple trees:

🌲 = 2 trees

There are 6 apple trees in Naomi's yard. How many tree symbols should Naomi use to show 6 apple trees?

Ⓐ 3
Ⓑ 2
Ⓒ 12
Ⓓ 6

40 Lydia eats 2 pieces of fruit every day. Which table shows how many pieces of fruit Lydia eats in 5, 7, and 14 days?

Ⓐ
Number of Days	Number of Pieces of Fruit
5	10
7	14
14	18

Ⓑ
Number of Days	Number of Pieces of Fruit
5	10
7	14
14	20

Ⓒ
Number of Days	Number of Pieces of Fruit
5	10
7	15
14	30

Ⓓ
Number of Days	Number of Pieces of Fruit
5	10
7	14
14	28

41 A recipe for meatballs calls for $\frac{1}{2}$ teaspoon of cumin. Which fraction is equivalent to $\frac{1}{2}$?

Ⓐ $\frac{2}{6}$

Ⓑ $\frac{2}{4}$

Ⓒ $\frac{4}{6}$

Ⓓ $\frac{3}{2}$

42 The picture below represents a playground.

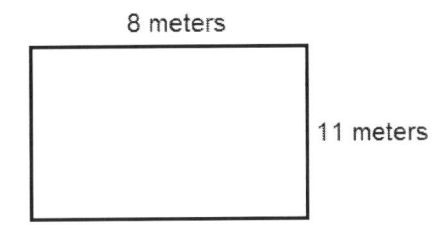

8 meters
11 meters

What is the perimeter of the playground?

Ⓐ 19 meters

Ⓑ 38 meters

Ⓒ 57 meters

Ⓓ 88 meters

43 Which of the following describes every rhombus?

Ⓐ   2 pairs of perpendicular sides

Ⓑ   4 right angles

Ⓒ   4 acute angles

Ⓓ   4 congruent sides

44 Which fraction model is equivalent to $\frac{1}{4}$?

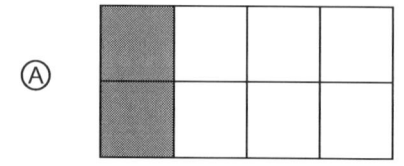

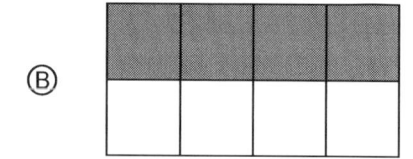

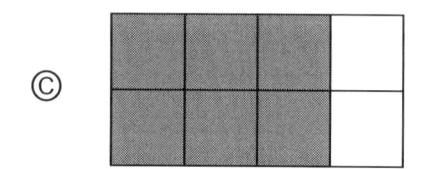

Ⓐ

Ⓑ

Ⓒ

Ⓓ

45 What part of the model is shaded?

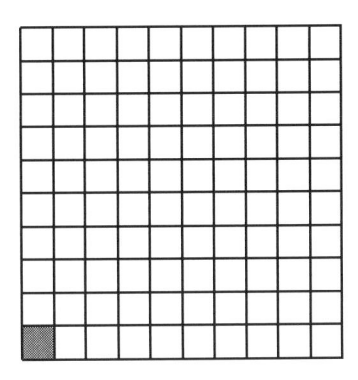

Ⓐ $\frac{1}{10}$

Ⓑ $\frac{10}{1}$

Ⓒ $\frac{1}{100}$

Ⓓ $\frac{100}{1}$

46 A school has 7 school buses. Each bus can seat 48 students. What is the total number of students the buses can seat?

Ⓐ 266

Ⓑ 336

Ⓒ 288

Ⓓ 284

47 Janet made the shape below out of cardboard. How many more edges does the shape have than vertices?

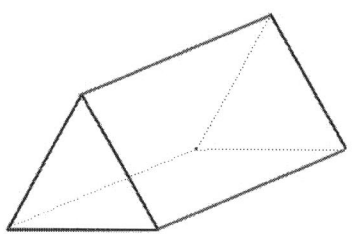

Ⓐ 1
Ⓑ 3
Ⓒ 4
Ⓓ 5

48 The graph below shows how far four students travel to school.

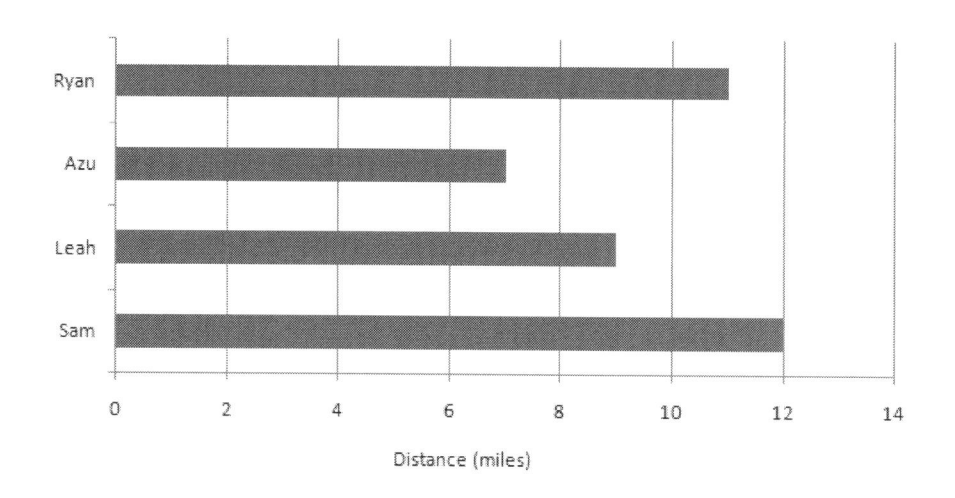

How much farther does Ryan travel than Azu?
Ⓐ 7 miles
Ⓑ 11 miles
Ⓒ 4 miles
Ⓓ 3 miles

49 Malcolm surveyed some people to find out how many pets they owned. The dot plot shows the results of the survey.

Number of Pets

```
                X
    X           X
    X           X
    X           X
    X           X       X
    X           X       X       X       X
    X           X       X       X       X
   _____
    0           1       2       3       4
```

How many people owned 2 or more pets?

Ⓐ 3
Ⓑ 4
Ⓒ 7
Ⓓ 9

50 The picture below represents a floor rug.

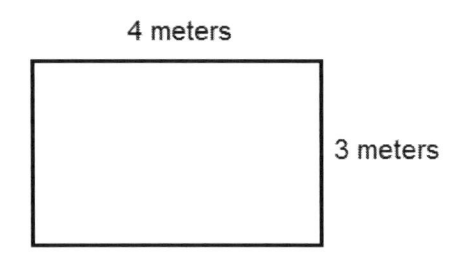

4 meters

3 meters

What is the perimeter of the floor rug?

Ⓐ 14 meters

Ⓑ 12 meters

Ⓒ 7 meters

Ⓓ 21 meters

51 Which of these shows a correct way of writing $\frac{2}{3}$?

Ⓐ $\frac{1}{3} \times \frac{1}{3} = \frac{2}{3}$

Ⓑ $\frac{1}{6} + \frac{1}{6} = \frac{2}{3}$

Ⓒ $\frac{1}{3} + \frac{1}{3} = \frac{2}{3}$

Ⓓ $\frac{1}{6} \times \frac{1}{6} = \frac{2}{3}$

52 A teacher divided 15 girls into 3 groups. How many girls were in each group?

Record your answer and fill in the bubbles on the grid. Be sure to use the correct place value.

53 A square garden has side lengths of 8 inches. What is the area of the garden?

Ⓐ 32 square inches

Ⓑ 36 square inches

Ⓒ 48 square inches

Ⓓ 64 square inches

54 Which fraction is represented by point *X*?

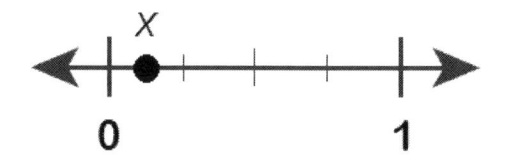

Ⓐ $\frac{1}{3}$

Ⓑ $\frac{1}{4}$

Ⓒ $\frac{1}{5}$

Ⓓ $\frac{1}{8}$

55 Mrs. Anderson took out a loan that will take her 60 months to pay off. How many years will it take Mrs. Anderson to pay off the loan?

> 1 year = 12 months

- Ⓐ 3 years
- Ⓑ 4 years
- Ⓒ 5 years
- Ⓓ 6 years

56 A pet shop sells fish for $3 each. How many fish does the pet shop need to sell to make $96?

- Ⓐ 32
- Ⓑ 36
- Ⓒ 48
- Ⓓ 288

57 What is the area of the shaded rectangle on the grid below, in square units?

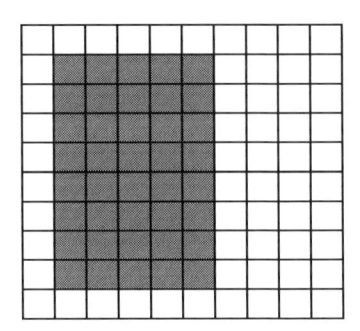

Record your answer and fill in the bubbles on the grid. Be sure to use the correct place value.

58 The shaded model below represents a fraction.

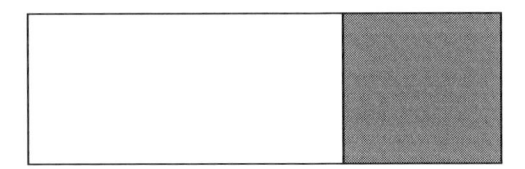

Which model below represents an equivalent fraction?

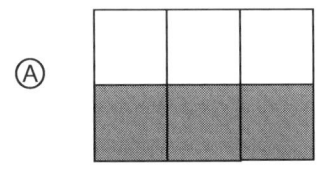

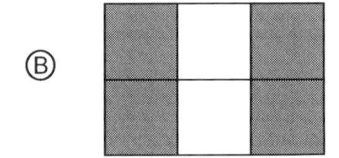

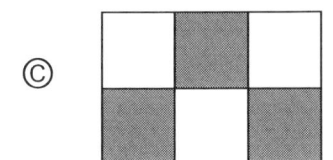

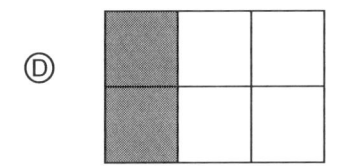

Ⓐ

Ⓑ

Ⓒ

Ⓓ

59 Which number makes the number sentence below true?

$$18 \div \square = 2$$

- Ⓐ 20
- Ⓑ 6
- Ⓒ 9
- Ⓓ 16

60 Lawson wants to buy a camera that costs $120. He earns $8 per week by doing chores. If Lawson saves all his money, how many weeks will it take him to save $120?

- Ⓐ 12 weeks
- Ⓑ 15 weeks
- Ⓒ 18 weeks
- Ⓓ 20 weeks

END OF TEST

STAAR Mathematics

Grade 3

Practice Test 3

Session 1

Directions

Read each question carefully. For a multiple-choice question, determine the best answer to the question from the four answer choices provided.

For a griddable question, determine the best answer. Write your answer at the top of the grid. Then shade the grid to show your answer.

You may use a ruler to help you answer questions. You may also use the information on the Reference Sheet at the back of this book. You may not use a calculator on this test.

1. A bookstore sold 40,905 books in May. Which of these is another way to write 40,905?

    Ⓐ   Four thousand nine hundred and five

    Ⓑ   Forty thousand ninety five

    Ⓒ   Four thousand ninety five

    Ⓓ   Forty thousand nine hundred and five

2. Which of the following shapes is a pentagon?

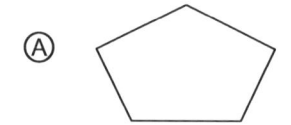

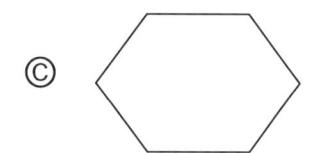

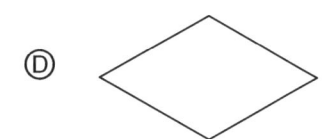

    Ⓐ

    Ⓑ

    Ⓒ

    Ⓓ

3 Which point on the number line represents 46?

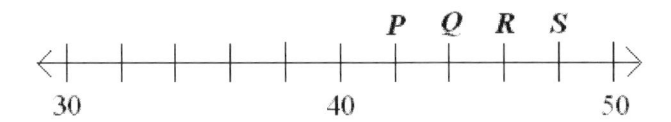

```
            P   Q   R   S
<—+—+—+—+—+—+—+—+—+—+—>
  30          40          50
```

- Ⓐ Point *P*
- Ⓑ Point *Q*
- Ⓒ Point *R*
- Ⓓ Point *S*

4 Sam read 39 pages of a novel in one week. He had 165 pages left to read. How many pages does the novel have?

- Ⓐ 204
- Ⓑ 136
- Ⓒ 194
- Ⓓ 126

5   Which number has a 3 in the thousands place?

   Ⓐ   10,386

   Ⓑ   35,689

   Ⓒ   23,782

   Ⓓ   71,935

6   Leonie has 20 books. She placed an equal number of books on 5 different shelves. There were no books left over.

   Which number sentence shows how many books Leonie put on each shelf?

   Ⓐ   20 + 5 = 25

   Ⓑ   20 − 5 = 15

   Ⓒ   20 × 5 = 100

   Ⓓ   20 ÷ 5 = 4

7 Which of the following has $\frac{1}{3}$ of the stars shaded?

Ⓐ

Ⓑ

Ⓒ

Ⓓ

8 The grid below represents 4 x 7.

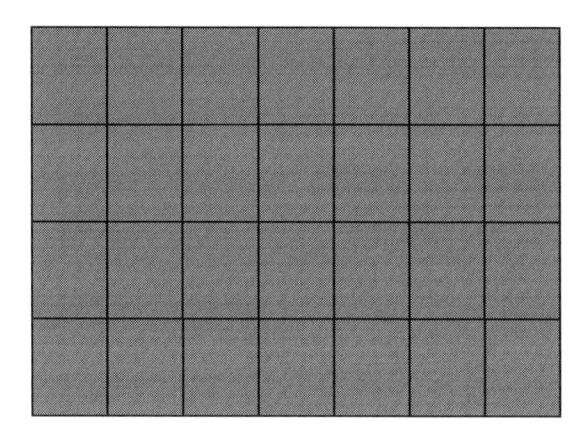

Which of these is another way to represent 4 x 7?

Ⓐ   7 + 7 + 7 + 7

Ⓑ   7 + 7 + 7 + 7 + 7 + 7 + 7

Ⓒ   4 + 4 + 4 + 4

Ⓓ   4 x 4 x 4 x 4

9 Each square on the grid below measures 1 cm by 1 cm.

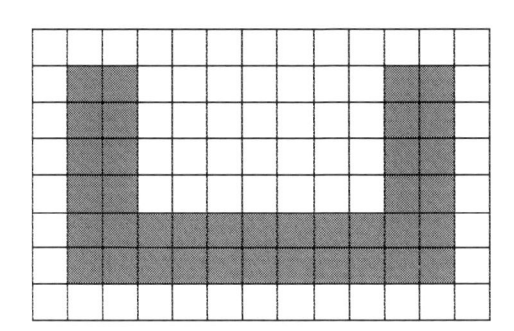

What is the area of the shaded figure, in square centimeters? Record your answer and fill in the bubbles on the grid. Be sure to use the correct place value.

10 Dannii is training for a bike race. She rode 17 miles on Monday, 19 miles on Tuesday, and 11 miles on Wednesday. Which is the best estimate of how far Dannii rode in all?

Ⓐ   30 miles

Ⓑ   40 miles

Ⓒ   50 miles

Ⓓ   60 miles

11 Gregory divided a rectangular piece of cardboard into sections, as shown below.

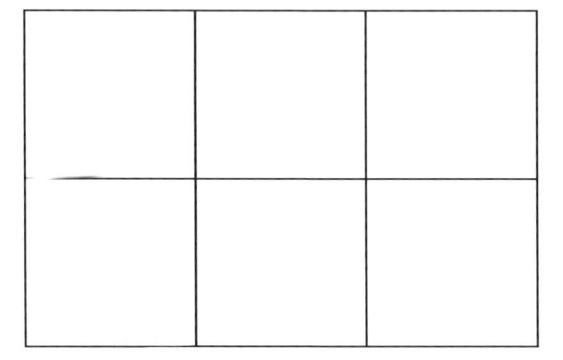

What fraction of the whole is each section?

Ⓐ $\frac{1}{2}$

Ⓑ $\frac{1}{3}$

Ⓒ $\frac{1}{5}$

Ⓓ $\frac{1}{6}$

12 Damon rode 3 miles to school every morning, and 3 miles back home each afternoon. How many miles would he ride in 5 days?

Ⓐ   15 miles

Ⓑ   30 miles

Ⓒ   45 miles

Ⓓ   60 miles

13 Which two shapes have the same number of sides?

Ⓐ   Triangle and rectangle

Ⓑ   Rectangle and square

Ⓒ   Hexagon and pentagon

Ⓓ   Pentagon and triangle

14 Which number goes in the box to make the equation below true?

$$\boxed{} \div 4 = 7$$

Ⓐ   3

Ⓑ   11

Ⓒ   21

Ⓓ   28

15. Davis, Trevor, and Ali each counted their savings. Davis had twice as much as Trevor and $2 more than Ali. Which of these could be how much they each had in savings?

    Ⓐ Davis $12, Trevor $6, Ali $10

    Ⓑ Davis $14, Trevor $7, Ali $16

    Ⓒ Davis $8, Trevor $16, Ali $6

    Ⓓ Davis $10, Trevor $20, Ali $12

16. What are the two smallest numbers that can be made using the digits 1, 6, and 4? Each digit must be used only once in each number.

    Ⓐ 146 and 164

    Ⓑ 146 and 416

    Ⓒ 614 and 641

    Ⓓ 416 and 164

17. The school library has 1,532 fiction books, 1,609 non-fiction books, and 1,239 children's books. Which number sentence shows the best way to estimate the total number of books?

    Ⓐ 1,500 + 1,600 + 1,200 = 4,300

    Ⓑ 1,500 + 1,600 + 1,300 = 4,400

    Ⓒ 1,600 + 1,600 + 1,300 = 4,500

    Ⓓ 1,600 + 1,700 + 1,300 = 4,600

18 Jennifer painted the eggs below for a craft project.

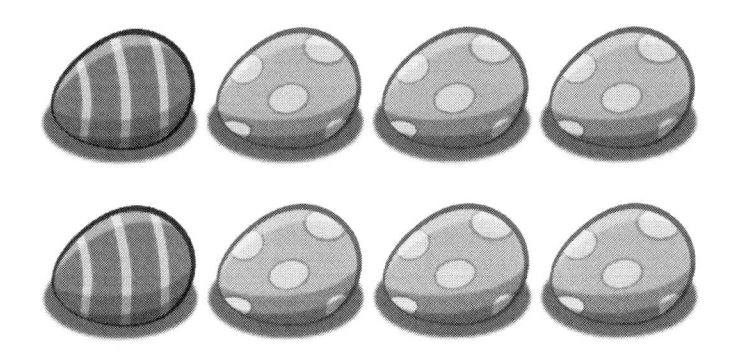

What fraction of the eggs are striped?

Ⓐ $\frac{1}{2}$

Ⓑ $\frac{1}{3}$

Ⓒ $\frac{1}{8}$

Ⓓ $\frac{1}{4}$

19 Which of these is the best estimate of the mass of a lemon?

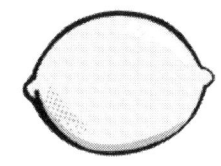

Ⓐ 2 ounces

Ⓑ 2 pounds

Ⓒ 2 ton

Ⓓ 2 kilograms

20 Which point on the number line represents $2\frac{1}{4}$?

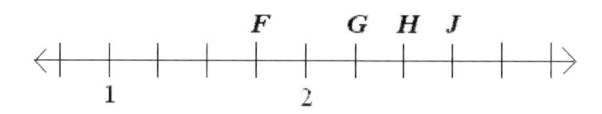

- Ⓐ Point *F*
- Ⓑ Point *G*
- Ⓒ Point *H*
- Ⓓ Point *J*

21 Which of these is the best estimate of the mass of a watermelon?

- Ⓐ 5 ounces
- Ⓑ 5 grams
- Ⓒ 5 pounds
- Ⓓ 5 milligrams

22 Which regular polygon would have a side length of 3 inches and a perimeter of 18 inches?

- Ⓐ Hexagon
- Ⓑ Square
- Ⓒ Pentagon
- Ⓓ Triangle

23 What is the product of 4 and 12? Record your answer and fill in the bubbles on the grid. Be sure to use the correct place value.

24 Which number sentence represents the array shown below?

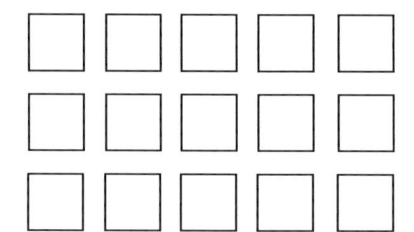

- Ⓐ $5 + 3 = 8$
- Ⓑ $5 \times 3 = 15$
- Ⓒ $15 \times 3 = 45$
- Ⓓ $20 - 5 = 15$

25 What is the perimeter of the rectangle below?

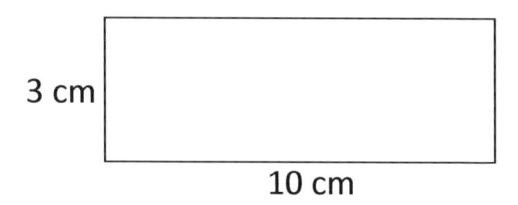

3 cm
10 cm

- Ⓐ 13 cm
- Ⓑ 30 cm
- Ⓒ 26 cm
- Ⓓ 60 cm

26   Which solid has the most congruent faces?

   Ⓐ   Cylinder

   Ⓑ   Cube

   Ⓒ   Triangular prism

   Ⓓ   Square pyramid

27   Tomato plants were planted in rows. Each row had the same number of tomato plants.

Number of Rows	Number of Tomato Plants
3	24
4	32
5	40
6	48

Based on the table above, how many tomato plants were in each row?

   Ⓐ   24
   Ⓑ   8
   Ⓒ   6
   Ⓓ   10

28 Rima is saving to buy a CD. The money she has saved so far is shown below. How much money has Rima saved?

Ⓐ $5.37

Ⓑ $5.62

Ⓒ $5.67

Ⓓ $5.92

29 Melinda buys bagels in packets of 4.

If Melinda counts the bagels in groups of 4, which number could she count?

Ⓐ   12

Ⓑ   10

Ⓒ   15

Ⓓ   18

30 Tim scored 21 points in a basketball game. Emmett scored 7 more points than Tim. Which method can be used to find how many points Tim and Emmett scored together?

Ⓐ   Add 21 and 7

Ⓑ   Add 21 to the sum of 21 and 7

Ⓒ   Add 21 to the difference of 21 and 7

Ⓓ   Subtract 7 from 21

END OF SESSION 1

STAAR Mathematics

Grade 3

Practice Test 3

Session 2

Directions

Read each question carefully. For a multiple-choice question, determine the best answer to the question from the four answer choices provided.

For a griddable question, determine the best answer. Write your answer at the top of the grid. Then shade the grid to show your answer.

You may use a ruler to help you answer questions. You may also use the information on the Reference Sheet at the back of this book. You may not use a calculator on this test.

31 A movie made $5,256,374 in its first weekend. What does the 2 in this number represent?

Ⓐ Two thousand

Ⓑ Twenty thousand

Ⓒ Two hundred thousand

Ⓓ Two million

32 Errol is putting photos into albums. Each album has 24 pages for holding photos, and each page can hold 8 photographs. How many photographs could Errol put into 3 photo albums? Record your answer and fill in the bubbles on the grid. Be sure to use the correct place value.

33 Which shape has exactly 5 sides?

Ⓐ   Square

Ⓑ   Hexagon

Ⓒ   Octagon

Ⓓ   Pentagon

34 There are 28 students at basketball training. The coach needs to divide the students into groups. Each group must have the same number of students in it. There cannot be any students left over. Which of the following could describe the groups?

Ⓐ   7 groups of 4 students

Ⓑ   8 groups of 3 students

Ⓒ   6 groups of 4 students

Ⓓ   10 groups of 3 students

35 Annie collects baseball cards. She has 22 cards in her collection. She gave her sister 2 baseball cards. Then Annie bought 4 new baseball cards. Which expression can be used to find the number of baseball cards Annie has now?

Ⓐ 22 + 2 + 4

Ⓑ 22 + 2 − 4

Ⓒ 22 − 2 + 4

Ⓓ 22 − 2 − 4

36 Which of these is equal to $\frac{1}{8} + \frac{1}{8} + \frac{1}{8}$?

Ⓐ $\frac{3}{8}$

Ⓑ $\frac{1}{512}$

Ⓒ $\frac{1}{24}$

Ⓓ $\frac{3}{24}$

37 The pictograph below shows how long Tamika spent at the computer each week day.

Monday	🖥🖥🖥🖥
Tuesday	🖥🖥🖥🖥🖥🖥
Wednesday	🖥🖥🖥🖥🖥
Thursday	🖥🖥🖥
Friday	🖥🖥

Each 🖥 means 10 minutes.

How long did Tamika spend at the computer on Wednesday?

Ⓐ 15 minutes

Ⓑ 60 minutes

Ⓒ 5 minutes

Ⓓ 50 minutes

38 A play sold $222 worth of tickets. Each ticket cost the same amount. Which of these could be the cost of each ticket?

Ⓐ $6

Ⓑ $8

Ⓒ $12

Ⓓ $16

39 Ming is making a pictograph to show how many boys are in grade 3, grade 4, and grade 5. The pictograph she has made so far is shown below.

Grade 3	☺☺☺☺☺☺
Grade 4	☺☺☺☺☺☺☺
Grade 5	

Each ☺ means 5 boys.

There are 50 boys in grade 5. Which of the following shows what Ming should put in the grade 5 row of the pictograph?

Ⓐ ☺☺☺☺☺

Ⓑ ☺☺☺☺☺☺☺

Ⓒ ☺☺☺☺☺☺☺☺☺

Ⓓ ☺☺☺☺☺☺☺☺☺☺

40   Lei jogs for 15 minutes every day. Which table shows how long Lei jogs for in 4, 5, and 6 days?

Ⓐ
Number of Days	Number of Minutes Jogged
4	60
5	65
6	70

Ⓑ
Number of Days	Number of Minutes Jogged
4	60
5	90
6	120

Ⓒ
Number of Days	Number of Minutes Jogged
4	15
5	30
6	45

Ⓓ
Number of Days	Number of Minutes Jogged
4	60
5	75
6	90

41 Dean drew these shapes.

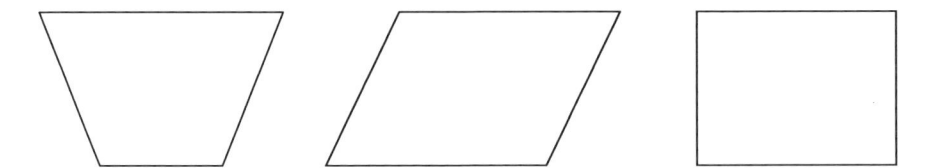

Salma drew these shapes.

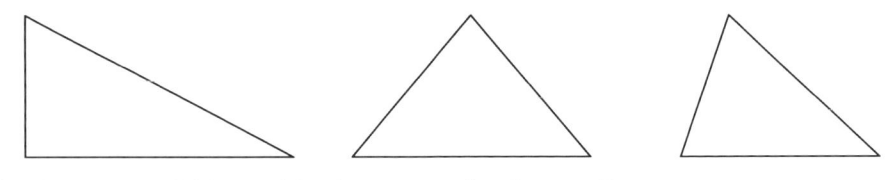

Which shape could be added to Dean's shapes?

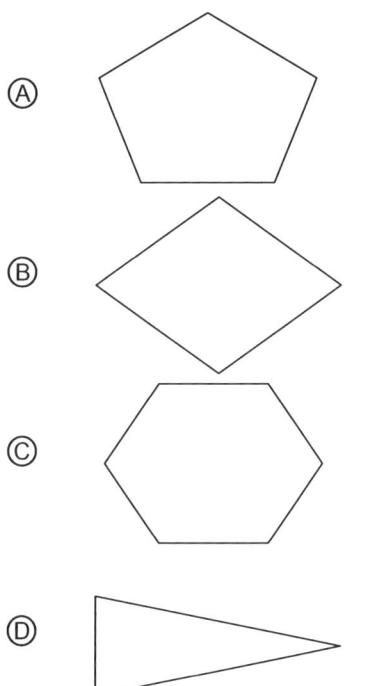

Ⓐ

Ⓑ

Ⓒ

Ⓓ

42 An array for the number 36 is shown below.

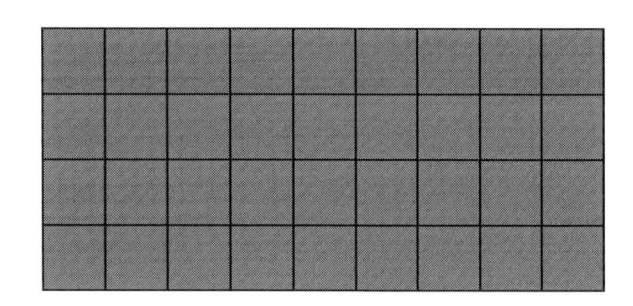

Which number can be divided evenly into 36?

Ⓐ 9
Ⓑ 8
Ⓒ 5
Ⓓ 7

43 A florist sells balloons in sets of 6. A customer ordered several sets of 6 balloons. Which of these could be the total number of balloons ordered?

Ⓐ 48
Ⓑ 50
Ⓒ 52
Ⓓ 56

44 Lee's singing lesson started at the time shown on the clock. If the lesson went for 45 minutes, what time did it end?

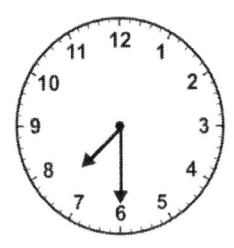

Ⓐ 7:30

Ⓑ 7:45

Ⓒ 8:15

Ⓓ 8:45

45 A piece of note paper has side lengths of 5 inches. What is the perimeter of the note paper?

Ⓐ 10 inches

Ⓑ 20 inches

Ⓒ 25 inches

Ⓓ 30 inches

46 Rita made the pictograph below to show how many cans each class collected for a food drive.

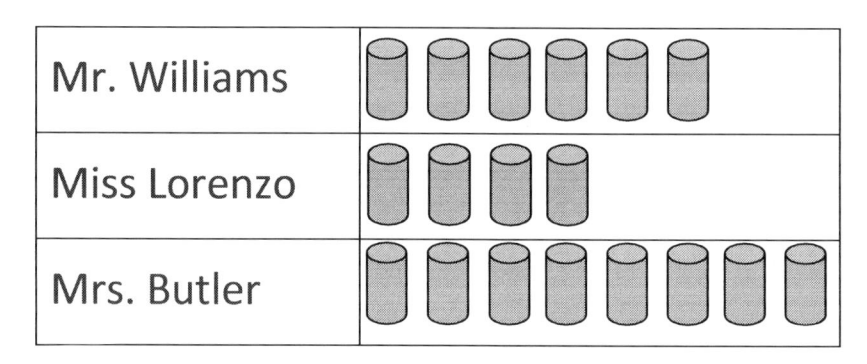

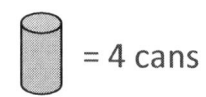

Mr. Williams	🥫🥫🥫🥫🥫
Miss Lorenzo	🥫🥫🥫
Mrs. Butler	🥫🥫🥫🥫🥫🥫🥫

🥫 = 4 cans

How many cans did Miss Lorenzo's class collect?

Ⓐ 4

Ⓑ 8

Ⓒ 16

Ⓓ 24

47 Which of these is the best estimate of the mass of an apple?

Ⓐ 100 milligrams

Ⓑ 100 grams

Ⓒ 100 kilograms

Ⓓ 100 tons

48 Kim is 63 inches tall. Chelsea is 4 inches taller than Kim. Vicky is 3 inches shorter than Chelsea. Which expression could be used to find Vicky's height, in inches?

- Ⓐ 63 − 4 − 3
- Ⓑ 63 + 4 + 3
- Ⓒ 63 − 4 + 3
- Ⓓ 63 + 4 − 3

49 What is the perimeter of the triangle shown below?

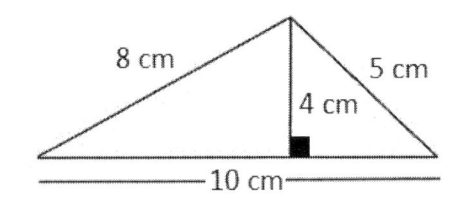

- Ⓐ 17 cm
- Ⓑ 19 cm
- Ⓒ 23 cm
- Ⓓ 27 cm

50 Kym is going camping. It costs $16 per night for the campsite. Kym plans to stay for 8 nights. How much will the campsite cost for 8 nights, in dollars? Record your answer and fill in the bubbles on the grid. Be sure to use the correct place value.

Practice Test Book, STAAR Math, Grade 3

51 Look at the shaded figure below.

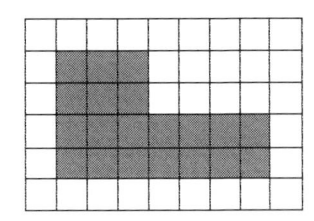

What is the area of the shaded figure?

Ⓐ   20 square units

Ⓑ   22 square units

Ⓒ   26 square units

Ⓓ   28 square units

52 The figure below models the number sentence 6 × 2 = 12.

Which number sentence is modeled by the same figure?

Ⓐ   6 ÷ 2 = 3

Ⓑ   36 ÷ 3 = 12

Ⓒ   12 ÷ 6 = 2

Ⓓ   24 ÷ 2 = 12

53 A square garden has side lengths of 8 inches. Jackie makes a rectangular garden with the same area as the square garden. Which of these could be the dimensions of the rectangular garden?

- Ⓐ 10 inches by 6 inches
- Ⓑ 7 inches by 9 inches
- Ⓒ 8 inches by 12 inches
- Ⓓ 16 inches by 4 inches

54 Which fraction is the greatest?

- Ⓐ $\dfrac{7}{10}$
- Ⓑ $\dfrac{4}{5}$
- Ⓒ $\dfrac{1}{5}$
- Ⓓ $\dfrac{9}{10}$

55 Nate plotted a fraction on the number line below.

Which fraction could Nate have been plotting?

Ⓐ $\dfrac{1}{2}$

Ⓑ $\dfrac{2}{2}$

Ⓒ $\dfrac{4}{2}$

Ⓓ $\dfrac{8}{2}$

56 Greg takes out a car loan for $20,000 with an interest rate of 10%. Which of these describes how much Greg will need to pay back to pay off the loan?

Ⓐ Less than $20,000

Ⓑ Exactly $20,000

Ⓒ Exactly $20,010

Ⓓ More than $20,000

57 Which number below is an odd number?

- Ⓐ   6
- Ⓑ   10
- Ⓒ   15
- Ⓓ   18

58 The normal price of a CD player is $298. During a sale, the CD player was $45 less than the normal price. What was the sale price of the CD player?

- Ⓐ $343
- Ⓑ $333
- Ⓒ $263
- Ⓓ $253

59 Look at the figure below.

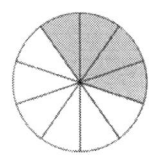

Which of these has the same fraction shaded?

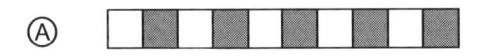

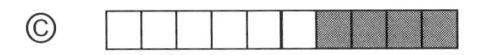

Ⓐ ▭▓▭▓▭▓▭▓

Ⓑ ▓▭▭▭▭▭▭▭

Ⓒ ▭▭▭▭▭▓▓▓

Ⓓ ▓▭▓▭▓▭▓

60 Fiona wants to have $600 in savings by the end of the year. If she saves the same amount each month, how much will she need to save each month to reach her goal?

Ⓐ $5

Ⓑ $15

Ⓒ $25

Ⓓ $50

END OF TEST

ANSWER KEY

About the Revised TEKS Standards

The STAAR Mathematics test assesses a specific set of skills. These are described in the Texas Essential Knowledge and Skills, or TEKS. Beginning with the 2014-2015 school year, student learning and assessment is based on the revised TEKS for mathematics. The questions in this book cover all the skills in the revised TEKS and will prepare students for the 2014-2015 STAAR assessments.

Reporting Categories and Skills

The TEKS standards are divided into four broad areas, known as Reporting Categories. On the state test, each category has a set amount of questions, with some categories having more questions than others. The Reporting Categories and the percentage of questions covering that category on the actual STAAR test are listed below.

Reporting Category	Percentage of Questions
Numerical Representations and Relationships	26%
Computations and Algebraic Relationships	39%
Geometry and Measurement	22%
Data Analysis and Personal Financial Literacy	13%

The answer key that follows includes the broad Reporting Category and the specific TEKS skill being assessed. These can be used to identify general areas of strength and weakness, as well as specific skills that the student is lacking. This information can then be used to target revision and instruction effectively.

STAAR Mathematics, Practice Test 1, Session 1

Question	Answer	Reporting Category	TEKS Skill
1	A	Numerical Representations and Relationships	Compose and decompose numbers up to 100,000 as a sum of so many ten thousands, so many thousands, so many hundreds, so many tens, and so many ones using objects, pictorial models, and numbers, including expanded notation as appropriate.
2	C	Data Analysis and Personal Financial Literacy	Solve one- and two-step problems using categorical data represented with a frequency table, dot plot, pictograph, or bar graph with scaled intervals.
3	A	Numerical Representations and Relationships	Compare two fractions having the same numerator or denominator in problems by reasoning about their sizes and justifying the conclusion using symbols, words, objects, and pictorial models.
4	D	Computations and Algebraic Relationships	Represent and solve one- and two-step multiplication and division problems within 100 using arrays, strip diagrams, and equations.
5	C	Numerical Representations and Relationships	Describe the mathematical relationships found in the base-10 place value system through the hundred thousands place.
6	C	Numerical Representations and Relationships	Solve problems involving partitioning an object or a set of objects among two or more recipients using pictorial representations of fractions with denominators of 2, 3, 4, 6, and 8.
7	D	Numerical Representations and Relationships	Represent equivalent fractions with denominators of 2, 3, 4, 6, and 8 using a variety of objects and pictorial models, including number lines.
8	17	Computations and Algebraic Relationships	Solve with fluency one-step and two-step problems involving addition and subtraction within 1,000 using strategies based on place value, properties of operations, and the relationship between addition and subtraction.
9	A	Geometry and Measurement	Decompose composite figures formed by rectangles into non-overlapping rectangles to determine the area of the original figure using the additive property of area.

10	C	Computations and Algebraic Relationships	Round to the nearest 10 or 100 or use compatible numbers to estimate solutions to addition and subtraction problems.
11	C	Geometry and Measurement	Use attributes to recognize rhombuses, parallelograms, trapezoids, rectangles, and squares as examples of quadrilaterals and draw examples of quadrilaterals that do not belong to any of these subcategories.
12	C	Computations and Algebraic Relationships	Describe a multiplication expression as a comparison such as 3 x 24 represents 3 times as much as 24.
13	6	Computations and Algebraic Relationships	Determine a quotient using the relationship between multiplication and division.
14	A	Geometry and Measurement	Classify and sort two- and three-dimensional figures, including cones, cylinders, spheres, triangular and rectangular prisms, and cubes, based on attributes using formal geometric language.
15	D	Geometry and Measurement	Determine when it is appropriate to use measurements of liquid volume (capacity) or weight.
16	C	Numerical Representations and Relationships	Describe the mathematical relationships found in the base-10 place value system through the hundred thousands place.
17	B	Computations and Algebraic Relationships	Round to the nearest 10 or 100 or use compatible numbers to estimate solutions to addition and subtraction problems.
18	B	Numerical Representations and Relationships	Represent fractions greater than zero and less than or equal to one with denominators of 2, 3, 4, 6, and 8 using concrete objects and pictorial models, including strip diagrams and number lines.
19	C	Computations and Algebraic Relationships	Represent multiplication facts by using a variety of approaches such as repeated addition, equal-sized groups, arrays, area models, equal jumps on a number line, and skip counting.
20	D	Numerical Representations and Relationships	Determine the corresponding fraction greater than zero and less than or equal to one with denominators of 2, 3, 4, 6, and 8 given a specified point on a number line.
21	C	Geometry and Measurement	Determine liquid volume (capacity) or weight using appropriate units and tools.

22	A	Computations and Algebraic Relationships	Recall facts to multiply up to 10 by 10 with automaticity and recall the corresponding division facts.
23	C	Geometry and Measurement	Classify and sort two- and three-dimensional figures, including cones, cylinders, spheres, triangular and rectangular prisms, and cubes, based on attributes using formal geometric language.
24	C	Geometry and Measurement	Determine the perimeter of a polygon or a missing length when given perimeter and remaining side lengths in problems.
25	D	Geometry and Measurement	Determine the area of rectangles with whole number side lengths in problems using multiplication related to the number of rows times the number of unit squares in each row.
26	B	Numerical Representations and Relationships	Determine if a number is even or odd using divisibility rules.
27	C	Computations and Algebraic Relationships	Represent real-world relationships using number pairs in a table and verbal descriptions.
28	B	Data Analysis and Personal Financial Literacy	Determine the value of a collection of coins and bills.
29	B	Computations and Algebraic Relationships	Solve one-step and two-step problems involving multiplication and division within 100 using strategies based on objects; pictorial models, including arrays, area models, and equal groups; properties of operations; or recall of facts.
30	A	Computations and Algebraic Relationships	Represent and solve one- and two-step multiplication and division problems within 100 using arrays, strip diagrams, and equations.

STAAR Mathematics, Practice Test 1, Session 2

Question	Answer	Reporting Category	TEKS Skill
31	A	Computations and Algebraic Relationships	Determine a quotient using the relationship between multiplication and division.
32	C	Data Analysis and Personal Financial Literacy	Summarize a data set with multiple categories using a frequency table, dot plot, pictograph, or bar graph with scaled intervals.
33	C	Numerical Representations and Relationships	Explain that two fractions are equivalent if and only if they are both represented by the same point on the number line or represent the same portion of a same size whole for an area model.
34	D	Computations and Algebraic Relationships	Solve one-step and two-step problems involving multiplication and division within 100 using strategies based on objects; pictorial models, including arrays, area models, and equal groups; properties of operations; or recall of facts.
35	D	Computations and Algebraic Relationships	Represent one- and two-step problems involving addition and subtraction of whole numbers to 1,000 using pictorial models, number lines, and equations.
36	B	Numerical Representations and Relationships	Represent a number on a number line as being between two consecutive multiples of 10; 100; 1,000; or 10,000 and use words to describe relative size of numbers in order to round whole numbers.
37	A	Data Analysis and Personal Financial Literacy	Summarize a data set with multiple categories using a frequency table, dot plot, pictograph, or bar graph with scaled intervals.
38	B	Geometry and Measurement	Determine the solutions to problems involving addition and subtraction of time intervals in minutes using pictorial models or tools such as a 15-minute event plus a 30-minute event equals 45 minutes.
39	B	Data Analysis and Personal Financial Literacy	Summarize a data set with multiple categories using a frequency table, dot plot, pictograph, or bar graph with scaled intervals.
40	A	Computations and Algebraic Relationships	Represent real-world relationships using number pairs in a table and verbal descriptions.

41	B	Data Analysis and Personal Financial Literacy	Solve one- and two-step problems using categorical data represented with a frequency table, dot plot, pictograph, or bar graph with scaled intervals.
42	72	Computations and Algebraic Relationships	Recall facts to multiply up to 10 by 10 with automaticity and recall the corresponding division facts.
43	D	Numerical Representations and Relationships	Compare and order whole numbers up to 100,000 and represent comparisons using the symbols >, <, or =.
44	B	Computations and Algebraic Relationships	Solve with fluency one-step and two-step problems involving addition and subtraction within 1,000 using strategies based on place value, properties of operations, and the relationship between addition and subtraction.
45	B	Geometry and Measurement	Determine the solutions to problems involving addition and subtraction of time intervals in minutes using pictorial models or tools such as a 15-minute event plus a 30-minute event equals 45 minutes.
46	A	Geometry and Measurement	Decompose composite figures formed by rectangles into non-overlapping rectangles to determine the area of the original figure using the additive property of area.
47	A	Numerical Representations and Relationships	Represent equivalent fractions with denominators of 2, 3, 4, 6, and 8 using a variety of objects and pictorial models, including number lines.
48	13	Data Analysis and Personal Financial Literacy	Summarize a data set with multiple categories using a frequency table, dot plot, pictograph, or bar graph with scaled intervals.
49	D	Geometry and Measurement	Use attributes to recognize rhombuses, parallelograms, trapezoids, rectangles, and squares as examples of quadrilaterals and draw examples of quadrilaterals that do not belong to any of these subcategories.
50	D	Numerical Representations and Relationships	Explain that the unit fraction $1/b$ represents the quantity formed by one part of a whole that has been partitioned into b equal parts where b is a non-zero whole number.
51	A	Numerical Representations and Relationships	Compose and decompose a fraction a/b with a numerator greater than zero and less than or equal to b as a sum of parts $1/b$.

52	B	Computations and Algebraic Relationships	Determine the unknown whole number in a multiplication or division equation relating three whole numbers when the unknown is either a missing factor or product.
53	B	Numerical Representations and Relationships	Represent fractions of halves, fourths, and eighths as distances from zero on a number line.
54	A	Computations and Algebraic Relationships	Use strategies and algorithms, including the standard algorithm, to multiply a two-digit number by a one-digit number. Strategies may include mental math, partial products, and the commutative, associative, and distributive properties.
55	C	Data Analysis and Personal Financial Literacy	Explain the connection between human capital/labor and income.
56	A	Numerical Representations and Relationships	Determine if a number is even or odd using divisibility rules.
57	B	Geometry and Measurement	Classify and sort two- and three-dimensional figures, including cones, cylinders, spheres, triangular and rectangular prisms, and cubes, based on attributes using formal geometric language.
58	A	Geometry and Measurement	Determine when it is appropriate to use measurements of liquid volume (capacity) or weight.
59	C	Data Analysis and Personal Financial Literacy	Determine the value of a collection of coins and bills.
60	B	Data Analysis and Personal Financial Literacy	Explain the connection between human capital/labor and income.

STAAR Mathematics, Practice Test 2, Session 1

Question	Answer	Reporting Category	TEKS Skill
1	A	Numerical Representations and Relationships	Compose and decompose numbers up to 100,000 as a sum of so many ten thousands, so many thousands, so many hundreds, so many tens, and so many ones using objects, pictorial models, and numbers, including expanded notation as appropriate.
2	C	Data Analysis and Personal Financial Literacy	Solve one- and two-step problems using categorical data represented with a frequency table, dot plot, pictograph, or bar graph with scaled intervals.
3	D	Numerical Representations and Relationships	Represent a number on a number line as being between two consecutive multiples of 10; 100; 1,000; or 10,000 and use words to describe relative size of numbers in order to round whole numbers.
4	B	Computations and Algebraic Relationships	Solve with fluency one-step and two-step problems involving addition and subtraction within 1,000 using strategies based on place value, properties of operations, and the relationship between addition and subtraction.
5	A	Numerical Representations and Relationships	Describe the mathematical relationships found in the base-10 place value system through the hundred thousands place.
6	B	Computations and Algebraic Relationships	Represent and solve one- and two-step multiplication and division problems within 100 using arrays, strip diagrams, and equations.
7	D	Geometry and Measurement	Determine the solutions to problems involving addition and subtraction of time intervals in minutes using pictorial models or tools such as a 15-minute event plus a 30-minute event equals 45 minutes.
8	C	Computations and Algebraic Relationships	Represent and solve one- and two-step multiplication and division problems within 100 using arrays, strip diagrams, and equations.
9	A	Geometry and Measurement	Decompose composite figures formed by rectangles into non-overlapping rectangles to determine the area of the original figure using the additive property of area.

10	C	Computations and Algebraic Relationships	Round to the nearest 10 or 100 or use compatible numbers to estimate solutions to addition and subtraction problems.
11	47	Computations and Algebraic Relationships	Solve one-step and two-step problems involving multiplication and division within 100 using strategies based on objects; pictorial models, including arrays, area models, and equal groups; properties of operations; or recall of facts.
12	B	Computations and Algebraic Relationships	Solve one-step and two-step problems involving multiplication and division within 100 using strategies based on objects; pictorial models, including arrays, area models, and equal groups; properties of operations; or recall of facts.
13	B	Geometry and Measurement	Classify and sort two- and three-dimensional figures, including cones, cylinders, spheres, triangular and rectangular prisms, and cubes, based on attributes using formal geometric language.
14	C	Computations and Algebraic Relationships	Recall facts to multiply up to 10 by 10 with automaticity and recall the corresponding division facts.
15	A	Computations and Algebraic Relationships	Determine the unknown whole number in a multiplication or division equation relating three whole numbers when the unknown is either a missing factor or product.
16	A	Computations and Algebraic Relationships	Round to the nearest 10 or 100 or use compatible numbers to estimate solutions to addition and subtraction problems.
17	D	Computations and Algebraic Relationships	Solve with fluency one-step and two-step problems involving addition and subtraction within 1,000 using strategies based on place value, properties of operations, and the relationship between addition and subtraction.
18	B	Numerical Representations and Relationships	Represent fractions greater than zero and less than or equal to one with denominators of 2, 3, 4, 6, and 8 using concrete objects and pictorial models, including strip diagrams and number lines.
19	B	Data Analysis and Personal Financial Literacy	Describe the relationship between the availability or scarcity of resources and how that impacts cost.

20	A	Numerical Representations and Relationships	Determine the corresponding fraction greater than zero and less than or equal to one with denominators of 2, 3, 4, 6, and 8 given a specified point on a number line.
21	B	Geometry and Measurement	Classify and sort two- and three-dimensional figures, including cones, cylinders, spheres, triangular and rectangular prisms, and cubes, based on attributes using formal geometric language.
22	B	Computations and Algebraic Relationships	Determine a quotient using the relationship between multiplication and division.
23	D	Geometry and Measurement	Use attributes to recognize rhombuses, parallelograms, trapezoids, rectangles, and squares as examples of quadrilaterals and draw examples of quadrilaterals that do not belong to any of these subcategories.
24	A	Numerical Representations and Relationships	Compose and decompose numbers up to 100,000 as a sum of so many ten thousands, so many thousands, so many hundreds, so many tens, and so many ones using objects, pictorial models, and numbers, including expanded notation as appropriate.
25	D	Geometry and Measurement	Determine the perimeter of a polygon or a missing length when given perimeter and remaining side lengths in problems.
26	B	Numerical Representations and Relationships	Represent a number on a number line as being between two consecutive multiples of 10; 100; 1,000; or 10,000 and use words to describe relative size of numbers in order to round whole numbers.
27	C	Computations and Algebraic Relationships	Represent real-world relationships using number pairs in a table and verbal descriptions.
28	A	Data Analysis and Personal Financial Literacy	Determine the value of a collection of coins and bills.
29	C	Computations and Algebraic Relationships	Determine the total number of objects when equally sized groups of objects are combined or arranged in arrays up to 10 by 10.
30	A	Numerical Representations and Relationships	Compare and order whole numbers up to 100,000 and represent comparisons using the symbols >, <, or =.

STAAR Mathematics, Practice Test 2, Session 2

Question	Answer	Reporting Category	TEKS Skill
31	B	Numerical Representations and Relationships	Compare and order whole numbers up to 100,000 and represent comparisons using the symbols >, <, or =.
32	D	Numerical Representations and Relationships	Determine if a number is even or odd using divisibility rules.
33	A	Numerical Representations and Relationships	Determine if a number is even or odd using divisibility rules.
34	C	Computations and Algebraic Relationships	Determine the number of objects in each group when a set of objects is partitioned into equal shares or a set of objects is shared equally.
35	A	Computations and Algebraic Relationships	Describe a multiplication expression as a comparison such as 3 x 24 represents 3 times as much as 24.
36	A	Computations and Algebraic Relationships	Solve with fluency one-step and two-step problems involving addition and subtraction within 1,000 using strategies based on place value, properties of operations, and the relationship between addition and subtraction.
37	A	Data Analysis and Personal Financial Literacy	Solve one- and two-step problems using categorical data represented with a frequency table, dot plot, pictograph, or bar graph with scaled intervals.
38	C	Computations and Algebraic Relationships	Use strategies and algorithms, including the standard algorithm, to multiply a two-digit number by a one-digit number. Strategies may include mental math, partial products, and the commutative, associative, and distributive properties.
39	A	Data Analysis and Personal Financial Literacy	Summarize a data set with multiple categories using a frequency table, dot plot, pictograph, or bar graph with scaled intervals.
40	D	Computations and Algebraic Relationships	Represent real-world relationships using number pairs in a table and verbal descriptions.

41	B	Numerical Representations and Relationships	Represent equivalent fractions with denominators of 2, 3, 4, 6, and 8 using a variety of objects and pictorial models, including number lines.
42	B	Geometry and Measurement	Determine the perimeter of a polygon or a missing length when given perimeter and remaining side lengths in problems.
43	D	Geometry and Measurement	Use attributes to recognize rhombuses, parallelograms, trapezoids, rectangles, and squares as examples of quadrilaterals and draw examples of quadrilaterals that do not belong to any of these subcategories.
44	A	Numerical Representations and Relationships	Explain that two fractions are equivalent if and only if they are both represented by the same point on the number line or represent the same portion of a same size whole for an area model.
45	C	Numerical Representations and Relationships	Explain that the unit fraction $1/b$ represents the quantity formed by one part of a whole that has been partitioned into b equal parts where b is a non-zero whole number.
46	B	Computations and Algebraic Relationships	Use strategies and algorithms, including the standard algorithm, to multiply a two-digit number by a one-digit number. Strategies may include mental math, partial products, and the commutative, associative, and distributive properties.
47	B	Geometry and Measurement	Classify and sort two- and three-dimensional figures, including cones, cylinders, spheres, triangular and rectangular prisms, and cubes, based on attributes using formal geometric language.
48	C	Data Analysis and Personal Financial Literacy	Solve one- and two-step problems using categorical data represented with a frequency table, dot plot, pictograph, or bar graph with scaled intervals.
49	C	Data Analysis and Personal Financial Literacy	Summarize a data set with multiple categories using a frequency table, dot plot, pictograph, or bar graph with scaled intervals.
50	A	Geometry and Measurement	Determine the perimeter of a polygon or a missing length when given perimeter and remaining side lengths in problems.

51	C	Numerical Representations and Relationships	Compose and decompose a fraction a/b with a numerator greater than zero and less than or equal to b as a sum of parts $1/b$.
52	5	Numerical Representations and Relationships	Solve problems involving partitioning an object or a set of objects among two or more recipients using pictorial representations of fractions with denominators of 2, 3, 4, 6, and 8.
53	D	Geometry and Measurement	Determine the area of rectangles with whole number side lengths in problems using multiplication related to the number of rows times the number of unit squares in each row.
54	D	Numerical Representations and Relationships	Represent fractions of halves, fourths, and eighths as distances from zero on a number line.
55	C	Data Analysis and Personal Financial Literacy	Explain that credit is used when wants or needs exceed the ability to pay and that it is the borrower's responsibility to pay it back to the lender, usually with interest.
56	A	Computations and Algebraic Relationships	Determine a quotient using the relationship between multiplication and division.
57	40	Geometry and Measurement	Determine the area of rectangles with whole number side lengths in problems using multiplication related to the number of rows times the number of unit squares in each row.
58	D	Numerical Representations and Relationships	Explain that two fractions are equivalent if and only if they are both represented by the same point on the number line or represent the same portion of a same size whole for an area model.
59	C	Computations and Algebraic Relationships	Determine the unknown whole number in a multiplication or division equation relating three whole numbers when the unknown is either a missing factor or product.
60	B	Data Analysis and Personal Financial Literacy	List reasons to save and explain the benefit of a savings plan, including for college.

STAAR Mathematics, Practice Test 3, Session 1

Question	Answer	Reporting Category	TEKS Skill
1	D	Numerical Representations and Relationships	Compose and decompose numbers up to 100,000 as a sum of so many ten thousands, so many thousands, so many hundreds, so many tens, and so many ones using objects, pictorial models, and numbers, including expanded notation as appropriate.
2	A	Geometry and Measurement	Classify and sort two- and three-dimensional figures, including cones, cylinders, spheres, triangular and rectangular prisms, and cubes, based on attributes using formal geometric language.
3	C	Numerical Representations and Relationships	Represent a number on a number line as being between two consecutive multiples of 10; 100; 1,000; or 10,000 and use words to describe relative size of numbers in order to round whole numbers.
4	A	Computations and Algebraic Relationships	Solve with fluency one-step and two-step problems involving addition and subtraction within 1,000 using strategies based on place value, properties of operations, and the relationship between addition and subtraction.
5	C	Numerical Representations and Relationships	Describe the mathematical relationships found in the base-10 place value system through the hundred thousands place.
6	D	Computations and Algebraic Relationships	Represent and solve one- and two-step multiplication and division problems within 100 using arrays, strip diagrams, and equations.
7	D	Numerical Representations and Relationships	Represent fractions greater than zero and less than or equal to one with denominators of 2, 3, 4, 6, and 8 using concrete objects and pictorial models, including strip diagrams and number lines.
8	A	Computations and Algebraic Relationships	Represent multiplication facts by using a variety of approaches such as repeated addition, equal-sized groups, arrays, area models, equal jumps on a number line, and skip counting.

9	38	Geometry and Measurement	Decompose composite figures formed by rectangles into non-overlapping rectangles to determine the area of the original figure using the additive property of area.
10	C	Computations and Algebraic Relationships	Round to the nearest 10 or 100 or use compatible numbers to estimate solutions to addition and subtraction problems.
11	D	Numerical Representations and Relationships	Explain that the unit fraction $1/b$ represents the quantity formed by one part of a whole that has been partitioned into b equal parts where b is a non-zero whole number.
12	B	Computations and Algebraic Relationships	Solve one-step and two-step problems involving multiplication and division within 100 using strategies based on objects; pictorial models, including arrays, area models, and equal groups; properties of operations; or recall of facts.
13	B	Geometry and Measurement	Classify and sort two- and three-dimensional figures, including cones, cylinders, spheres, triangular and rectangular prisms, and cubes, based on attributes using formal geometric language.
14	D	Computations and Algebraic Relationships	Determine the unknown whole number in a multiplication or division equation relating three whole numbers when the unknown is either a missing factor or product.
15	A	Computations and Algebraic Relationships	Represent real-world relationships using number pairs in a table and verbal descriptions.
16	A	Numerical Representations and Relationships	Describe the mathematical relationships found in the base-10 place value system through the hundred thousands place.
17	A	Computations and Algebraic Relationships	Round to the nearest 10 or 100 or use compatible numbers to estimate solutions to addition and subtraction problems.
18	D	Numerical Representations and Relationships	Represent fractions greater than zero and less than or equal to one with denominators of 2, 3, 4, 6, and 8 using concrete objects and pictorial models, including strip diagrams and number lines.
19	A	Geometry and Measurement	Determine liquid volume (capacity) or weight using appropriate units and tools.

20	B	Numerical Representations and Relationships	Determine the corresponding fraction greater than zero and less than or equal to one with denominators of 2, 3, 4, 6, and 8 given a specified point on a number line.
21	C	Geometry and Measurement	Determine liquid volume (capacity) or weight using appropriate units and tools.
22	A	Geometry and Measurement	Determine the perimeter of a polygon or a missing length when given perimeter and remaining side lengths in problems.
23	48	Computations and Algebraic Relationships	Use strategies and algorithms, including the standard algorithm, to multiply a two-digit number by a one-digit number. Strategies may include mental math, partial products, and the commutative, associative, and distributive properties.
24	B	Computations and Algebraic Relationships	Represent multiplication facts by using a variety of approaches such as repeated addition, equal-sized groups, arrays, area models, equal jumps on a number line, and skip counting.
25	C	Geometry and Measurement	Determine the perimeter of a polygon or a missing length when given perimeter and remaining side lengths in problems.
26	B	Geometry and Measurement	Classify and sort two- and three-dimensional figures, including cones, cylinders, spheres, triangular and rectangular prisms, and cubes, based on attributes using formal geometric language.
27	B	Computations and Algebraic Relationships	Represent real-world relationships using number pairs in a table and verbal descriptions.
28	C	Data Analysis and Personal Financial Literacy	Determine the value of a collection of coins and bills.
29	A	Computations and Algebraic Relationships	Represent multiplication facts by using a variety of approaches such as repeated addition, equal-sized groups, arrays, area models, equal jumps on a number line, and skip counting.
30	B	Computations and Algebraic Relationships	Solve with fluency one-step and two-step problems involving addition and subtraction within 1,000 using strategies based on place value, properties of operations, and the relationship between addition and subtraction.

STAAR Mathematics, Practice Test 3, Session 2

Question	Answer	Reporting Category	TEKS Skill
31	C	Numerical Representations and Relationships	Compose and decompose numbers up to 100,000 as a sum of so many ten thousands, so many thousands, so many hundreds, so many tens, and so many ones using objects, pictorial models, and numbers, including expanded notation as appropriate.
32	576	Computations and Algebraic Relationships	Represent and solve one- and two-step multiplication and division problems within 100 using arrays, strip diagrams, and equations.
33	D	Geometry and Measurement	Classify and sort two- and three-dimensional figures, including cones, cylinders, spheres, triangular and rectangular prisms, and cubes, based on attributes using formal geometric language.
34	A	Computations and Algebraic Relationships	Determine the total number of objects when equally sized groups of objects are combined or arranged in arrays up to 10 by 10.
35	C	Computations and Algebraic Relationships	Represent one- and two-step problems involving addition and subtraction of whole numbers to 1,000 using pictorial models, number lines, and equations.
36	A	Numerical Representations and Relationships	Compose and decompose a fraction a/b with a numerator greater than zero and less than or equal to b as a sum of parts $1/b$.
37	D	Data Analysis and Personal Financial Literacy	Solve one- and two-step problems using categorical data represented with a frequency table, dot plot, pictograph, or bar graph with scaled intervals.
38	A	Computations and Algebraic Relationships	Determine a quotient using the relationship between multiplication and division.
39	C	Data Analysis and Personal Financial Literacy	Summarize a data set with multiple categories using a frequency table, dot plot, pictograph, or bar graph with scaled intervals.
40	D	Computations and Algebraic Relationships	Represent real-world relationships using number pairs in a table and verbal descriptions.

41	B	Geometry and Measurement	Use attributes to recognize rhombuses, parallelograms, trapezoids, rectangles, and squares as examples of quadrilaterals and draw examples of quadrilaterals that do not belong to any of these subcategories.
42	A	Computations and Algebraic Relationships	Determine a quotient using the relationship between multiplication and division.
43	A	Computations and Algebraic Relationships	Solve one-step and two-step problems involving multiplication and division within 100 using strategies based on objects; pictorial models, including arrays, area models, and equal groups; properties of operations; or recall of facts.
44	C	Geometry and Measurement	Determine the solutions to problems involving addition and subtraction of time intervals in minutes using pictorial models or tools such as a 15-minute event plus a 30-minute event equals 45 minutes.
45	B	Geometry and Measurement	Determine the perimeter of a polygon or a missing length when given perimeter and remaining side lengths in problems.
46	C	Data Analysis and Personal Financial Literacy	Solve one- and two-step problems using categorical data represented with a frequency table, dot plot, pictograph, or bar graph with scaled intervals.
47	B	Geometry and Measurement	Determine liquid volume (capacity) or weight using appropriate units and tools.
48	D	Computations and Algebraic Relationships	Represent one- and two-step problems involving addition and subtraction of whole numbers to 1,000 using pictorial models, number lines, and equations.
49	C	Geometry and Measurement	Determine the perimeter of a polygon or a missing length when given perimeter and remaining side lengths in problems.
50	128	Computations and Algebraic Relationships	Use strategies and algorithms, including the standard algorithm, to multiply a two-digit number by a one-digit number. Strategies may include mental math, partial products, and the commutative, associative, and distributive properties.

51	A	Geometry and Measurement	Decompose composite figures formed by rectangles into non-overlapping rectangles to determine the area of the original figure using the additive property of area.
52	C	Computations and Algebraic Relationships	Determine a quotient using the relationship between multiplication and division.
53	D	Geometry and Measurement	Determine the area of rectangles with whole number side lengths in problems using multiplication related to the number of rows times the number of unit squares in each row.
54	D	Numerical Representations and Relationships	Compare two fractions having the same numerator or denominator in problems by reasoning about their sizes and justifying the conclusion using symbols, words, objects, and pictorial models.
55	C	Numerical Representations and Relationships	Explain that two fractions are equivalent if and only if they are both represented by the same point on the number line or represent the same portion of a same size whole for an area model.
56	D	Data Analysis and Personal Financial Literacy	Explain that credit is used when wants or needs exceed the ability to pay and that it is the borrower's responsibility to pay it back to the lender, usually with interest.
57	C	Numerical Representations and Relationships	Determine if a number is even or odd using divisibility rules.
58	D	Computations and Algebraic Relationships	Solve with fluency one-step and two-step problems involving addition and subtraction within 1,000 using strategies based on place value, properties of operations, and the relationship between addition and subtraction.
59	C	Geometry and Measurement	Decompose two congruent two-dimensional figures into parts with equal areas and express the area of each part as a unit fraction of the whole and recognize that equal shares of identical wholes need not have the same shape.
60	D	Data Analysis and Personal Financial Literacy	List reasons to save and explain the benefit of a savings plan, including for college.

Answer Sheet: Practice Test 1

Session 1

1	Ⓐ Ⓑ Ⓒ Ⓓ	11	Ⓐ Ⓑ Ⓒ Ⓓ	21	Ⓐ Ⓑ Ⓒ Ⓓ
2	Ⓐ Ⓑ Ⓒ Ⓓ	12	Ⓐ Ⓑ Ⓒ Ⓓ	22	Ⓐ Ⓑ Ⓒ Ⓓ
3	Ⓐ Ⓑ Ⓒ Ⓓ	13	_____	23	Ⓐ Ⓑ Ⓒ Ⓓ
4	Ⓐ Ⓑ Ⓒ Ⓓ	14	Ⓐ Ⓑ Ⓒ Ⓓ	24	Ⓐ Ⓑ Ⓒ Ⓓ
5	Ⓐ Ⓑ Ⓒ Ⓓ	15	Ⓐ Ⓑ Ⓒ Ⓓ	25	Ⓐ Ⓑ Ⓒ Ⓓ
6	Ⓐ Ⓑ Ⓒ Ⓓ	16	Ⓐ Ⓑ Ⓒ Ⓓ	26	Ⓐ Ⓑ Ⓒ Ⓓ
7	Ⓐ Ⓑ Ⓒ Ⓓ	17	Ⓐ Ⓑ Ⓒ Ⓓ	27	Ⓐ Ⓑ Ⓒ Ⓓ
8	_____	18	Ⓐ Ⓑ Ⓒ Ⓓ	28	Ⓐ Ⓑ Ⓒ Ⓓ
9	Ⓐ Ⓑ Ⓒ Ⓓ	19	Ⓐ Ⓑ Ⓒ Ⓓ	29	Ⓐ Ⓑ Ⓒ Ⓓ
10	Ⓐ Ⓑ Ⓒ Ⓓ	20	Ⓐ Ⓑ Ⓒ Ⓓ	30	Ⓐ Ⓑ Ⓒ Ⓓ

Session 2

31	Ⓐ Ⓑ Ⓒ Ⓓ	41	Ⓐ Ⓑ Ⓒ Ⓓ	51	Ⓐ Ⓑ Ⓒ Ⓓ
32	Ⓐ Ⓑ Ⓒ Ⓓ	42	_____	52	Ⓐ Ⓑ Ⓒ Ⓓ
33	Ⓐ Ⓑ Ⓒ Ⓓ	43	Ⓐ Ⓑ Ⓒ Ⓓ	53	Ⓐ Ⓑ Ⓒ Ⓓ
34	Ⓐ Ⓑ Ⓒ Ⓓ	44	Ⓐ Ⓑ Ⓒ Ⓓ	54	Ⓐ Ⓑ Ⓒ Ⓓ
35	Ⓐ Ⓑ Ⓒ Ⓓ	45	Ⓐ Ⓑ Ⓒ Ⓓ	55	Ⓐ Ⓑ Ⓒ Ⓓ
36	Ⓐ Ⓑ Ⓒ Ⓓ	46	Ⓐ Ⓑ Ⓒ Ⓓ	56	Ⓐ Ⓑ Ⓒ Ⓓ
37	Ⓐ Ⓑ Ⓒ Ⓓ	47	Ⓐ Ⓑ Ⓒ Ⓓ	57	Ⓐ Ⓑ Ⓒ Ⓓ
38	Ⓐ Ⓑ Ⓒ Ⓓ	48	_____	58	Ⓐ Ⓑ Ⓒ Ⓓ
39	Ⓐ Ⓑ Ⓒ Ⓓ	49	Ⓐ Ⓑ Ⓒ Ⓓ	59	Ⓐ Ⓑ Ⓒ Ⓓ
40	Ⓐ Ⓑ Ⓒ Ⓓ	50	Ⓐ Ⓑ Ⓒ Ⓓ	60	Ⓐ Ⓑ Ⓒ Ⓓ

Answer Sheet: Practice Test 2

Session 1

1	Ⓐ Ⓑ Ⓒ Ⓓ	11	_____	21	Ⓐ Ⓑ Ⓒ Ⓓ
2	Ⓐ Ⓑ Ⓒ Ⓓ	12	Ⓐ Ⓑ Ⓒ Ⓓ	22	Ⓐ Ⓑ Ⓒ Ⓓ
3	Ⓐ Ⓑ Ⓒ Ⓓ	13	Ⓐ Ⓑ Ⓒ Ⓓ	23	Ⓐ Ⓑ Ⓒ Ⓓ
4	Ⓐ Ⓑ Ⓒ Ⓓ	14	Ⓐ Ⓑ Ⓒ Ⓓ	24	Ⓐ Ⓑ Ⓒ Ⓓ
5	Ⓐ Ⓑ Ⓒ Ⓓ	15	Ⓐ Ⓑ Ⓒ Ⓓ	25	Ⓐ Ⓑ Ⓒ Ⓓ
6	Ⓐ Ⓑ Ⓒ Ⓓ	16	Ⓐ Ⓑ Ⓒ Ⓓ	26	Ⓐ Ⓑ Ⓒ Ⓓ
7	Ⓐ Ⓑ Ⓒ Ⓓ	17	Ⓐ Ⓑ Ⓒ Ⓓ	27	Ⓐ Ⓑ Ⓒ Ⓓ
8	Ⓐ Ⓑ Ⓒ Ⓓ	18	Ⓐ Ⓑ Ⓒ Ⓓ	28	Ⓐ Ⓑ Ⓒ Ⓓ
9	Ⓐ Ⓑ Ⓒ Ⓓ	19	Ⓐ Ⓑ Ⓒ Ⓓ	29	Ⓐ Ⓑ Ⓒ Ⓓ
10	Ⓐ Ⓑ Ⓒ Ⓓ	20	Ⓐ Ⓑ Ⓒ Ⓓ	30	Ⓐ Ⓑ Ⓒ Ⓓ

Session 2

31	Ⓐ Ⓑ Ⓒ Ⓓ	41	Ⓐ Ⓑ Ⓒ Ⓓ	51	Ⓐ Ⓑ Ⓒ Ⓓ
32	Ⓐ Ⓑ Ⓒ Ⓓ	42	Ⓐ Ⓑ Ⓒ Ⓓ	52	_____
33	Ⓐ Ⓑ Ⓒ Ⓓ	43	Ⓐ Ⓑ Ⓒ Ⓓ	53	Ⓐ Ⓑ Ⓒ Ⓓ
34	Ⓐ Ⓑ Ⓒ Ⓓ	44	Ⓐ Ⓑ Ⓒ Ⓓ	54	Ⓐ Ⓑ Ⓒ Ⓓ
35	Ⓐ Ⓑ Ⓒ Ⓓ	45	Ⓐ Ⓑ Ⓒ Ⓓ	55	Ⓐ Ⓑ Ⓒ Ⓓ
36	Ⓐ Ⓑ Ⓒ Ⓓ	46	Ⓐ Ⓑ Ⓒ Ⓓ	56	Ⓐ Ⓑ Ⓒ Ⓓ
37	Ⓐ Ⓑ Ⓒ Ⓓ	47	Ⓐ Ⓑ Ⓒ Ⓓ	57	_____
38	Ⓐ Ⓑ Ⓒ Ⓓ	48	Ⓐ Ⓑ Ⓒ Ⓓ	58	Ⓐ Ⓑ Ⓒ Ⓓ
39	Ⓐ Ⓑ Ⓒ Ⓓ	49	Ⓐ Ⓑ Ⓒ Ⓓ	59	Ⓐ Ⓑ Ⓒ Ⓓ
40	Ⓐ Ⓑ Ⓒ Ⓓ	50	Ⓐ Ⓑ Ⓒ Ⓓ	60	Ⓐ Ⓑ Ⓒ Ⓓ

Answer Sheet: Practice Test 3

Session 1

1	Ⓐ Ⓑ Ⓒ Ⓓ	11	Ⓐ Ⓑ Ⓒ Ⓓ	21	Ⓐ Ⓑ Ⓒ Ⓓ
2	Ⓐ Ⓑ Ⓒ Ⓓ	12	Ⓐ Ⓑ Ⓒ Ⓓ	22	Ⓐ Ⓑ Ⓒ Ⓓ
3	Ⓐ Ⓑ Ⓒ Ⓓ	13	Ⓐ Ⓑ Ⓒ Ⓓ	23	_____
4	Ⓐ Ⓑ Ⓒ Ⓓ	14	Ⓐ Ⓑ Ⓒ Ⓓ	24	Ⓐ Ⓑ Ⓒ Ⓓ
5	Ⓐ Ⓑ Ⓒ Ⓓ	15	Ⓐ Ⓑ Ⓒ Ⓓ	25	Ⓐ Ⓑ Ⓒ Ⓓ
6	Ⓐ Ⓑ Ⓒ Ⓓ	16	Ⓐ Ⓑ Ⓒ Ⓓ	26	Ⓐ Ⓑ Ⓒ Ⓓ
7	Ⓐ Ⓑ Ⓒ Ⓓ	17	Ⓐ Ⓑ Ⓒ Ⓓ	27	Ⓐ Ⓑ Ⓒ Ⓓ
8	Ⓐ Ⓑ Ⓒ Ⓓ	18	Ⓐ Ⓑ Ⓒ Ⓓ	28	Ⓐ Ⓑ Ⓒ Ⓓ
9	_____	19	Ⓐ Ⓑ Ⓒ Ⓓ	29	Ⓐ Ⓑ Ⓒ Ⓓ
10	Ⓐ Ⓑ Ⓒ Ⓓ	20	Ⓐ Ⓑ Ⓒ Ⓓ	30	Ⓐ Ⓑ Ⓒ Ⓓ

Session 2

31	Ⓐ Ⓑ Ⓒ Ⓓ	41	Ⓐ Ⓑ Ⓒ Ⓓ	51	Ⓐ Ⓑ Ⓒ Ⓓ
32	_____	42	Ⓐ Ⓑ Ⓒ Ⓓ	52	Ⓐ Ⓑ Ⓒ Ⓓ
33	Ⓐ Ⓑ Ⓒ Ⓓ	43	Ⓐ Ⓑ Ⓒ Ⓓ	53	Ⓐ Ⓑ Ⓒ Ⓓ
34	Ⓐ Ⓑ Ⓒ Ⓓ	44	Ⓐ Ⓑ Ⓒ Ⓓ	54	Ⓐ Ⓑ Ⓒ Ⓓ
35	Ⓐ Ⓑ Ⓒ Ⓓ	45	Ⓐ Ⓑ Ⓒ Ⓓ	55	Ⓐ Ⓑ Ⓒ Ⓓ
36	Ⓐ Ⓑ Ⓒ Ⓓ	46	Ⓐ Ⓑ Ⓒ Ⓓ	56	Ⓐ Ⓑ Ⓒ Ⓓ
37	Ⓐ Ⓑ Ⓒ Ⓓ	47	Ⓐ Ⓑ Ⓒ Ⓓ	57	Ⓐ Ⓑ Ⓒ Ⓓ
38	Ⓐ Ⓑ Ⓒ Ⓓ	48	Ⓐ Ⓑ Ⓒ Ⓓ	58	Ⓐ Ⓑ Ⓒ Ⓓ
39	Ⓐ Ⓑ Ⓒ Ⓓ	49	Ⓐ Ⓑ Ⓒ Ⓓ	59	Ⓐ Ⓑ Ⓒ Ⓓ
40	Ⓐ Ⓑ Ⓒ Ⓓ	50	_____	60	Ⓐ Ⓑ Ⓒ Ⓓ

STAAR Grade 3 Mathematics Reference Sheet

You may use this information to help you answer questions.

LENGTH

Customary
1 mile (mi) = 1,760 yards (yd)
1 yard (yd) = 3 feet (ft)
1 foot (ft) = 12 inches (in.)

Metric
1 kilometer (km) = 1,000 meters (m)
1 meter (m) = 100 centimeters (cm)
1 centimeter (cm) = 10 millimeters (mm)

VOLUME AND CAPACITY

Customary
1 gallon (gal) = 4 quarts (qt)
1 quart (qt) = 2 pints (pt)
1 pint (pt) = 2 cups (c)
1 cup (c) = 8 fluid ounces (fl oz)

Metric
1 liter (L) = 1,000 milliliters (mL)

WEIGHT AND MASS

Customary
1 ton (T) = 2,000 pounds (lb)
1 pound (lb) = 16 ounces (oz)

Metric
1 kilogram (kg) = 1,000 grams (g)
1 gram (g) = 1,000 milligrams (mg)

TIME

1 year = 12 months
1 year = 52 weeks
1 week = 7 days

1 day = 24 hours
1 hour = 60 minutes
1 minute = 60 seconds

Made in the USA
Lexington, KY
22 January 2015